STRUGGLE
FOR
INTIMACY

STRUGGLE FOR INTIMACY

Janet Geringer Woititz, Ed.D.

Health Communications, Inc.
Deerfield Beach, Florida

www.bcibooks.com

Library of Congress Cataloging-in-Publication Data

Woititz, Janet Geringer.
    Struggle for Intimacy / Janet G. Woititz
        p.   cm.
    ISBN-13: 978-0-932194-25-1
    ISBN-10: 0-932194-25-7

© 1990 Janet G. Woititz

Publisher: Health Communications, Inc.
            3201 S.W. 15th Street
            Deerfield Beach, FL 33442-8190

Cover redesign by Lawna Patterson Oldfield
Inside book redesign by Dawn Von Strolley Grove

This book is dedicated to those who struggle
for and with intimacy.
Although it is written to those of you
who grew up with substance abuse,
it is written for those who grew up
in other types of dysfunctional families as well.

CONTENTS

ACKNOWLEDGMENTS

To Dave, Lisa and Danny for their specialness. To my Monday Night Group—Dr. Don Gregg, Ken Kirkland, Andrea Becker, Bonnie White, Eileen Lindsay, Claudia O'Brien, Ed Ellis, Miriam Sender, Sue Falan and Bernie Zweben for their help.

To the "Super Brats" from my Adult Children of Alcoholics course at Rutgers Summer School for Alcohol Studies for their validation.

PREFACE

Several months have passed since I first made the commitment to write this book. It has been a great struggle to begin putting these thoughts on paper. If I considered myself a writer, I could call it "writer's block."

Since I consider myself a clinician, I know that there is something more to it.

For me, writing has been a compulsive act; when, for some reason, I find the words won't come, I need to look further. Writing *Marriage on the Rocks* happened so quickly and so easily that I wondered if I was really the one writing it. It was a cleansing act for me, and for others like me, and it served a purpose. When I wrote *Adult Children of Alcoholics*, I wrote that, too, with relative ease. I wrote it for my children—the hundreds of my children who have been part of my life and part of my counseling practice.

I felt confident when I wrote both of these books that I was answering some questions, providing some "how to's" that I knew would work.

To write about the struggle for intimacy is quite another matter. It is a much more complex issue, key to the happiness of every man and woman. It is quite clear to me that I am not as detached as I was when I wrote the other books. My own feelings are affected by the magnitude of this problem.

Maybe the reason I have had such a struggle in writing about intimacy is that I'm not sure this time that I can make things better for you. I think this book may help to clarify, but I am not so sure that it will heal you. What I do know is that the issues in this book need to be discussed in this context.

What I hope is that you are reading this book with the intent of airing some issues, so that wounds will be lanced and disinfected, knowing that they will then have the opportunity to heal. I am fearful that you will be disappointed if you expect to find *the one answer* in this book.

The struggle for intimacy goes on for all of us as long as we live. But it is especially difficult for those who have grown up with alcoholism. To be intimate, to be close, to be vulnerable, contradicts all the survival skills learned by Children of Alcoholics (COAs) when they were very young. Acquiring intimacy skills requires a complete relearning process and is, to say the least, a monumental task. Let us begin.

INTRODUCTION

Even though divorce statistics and the number of unhappy people we all know confirm that not only Adult Children of Alcoholics (COAs) struggle with relationships, those of you who fall into the COA category have some very special problems and very special needs.

Although the struggle for intimacy is not yours alone, the ways needed to fix the problems may be unique.

First, you were set up for the situation in which you now find yourself. You never had a chance to "do it right" because you've never experienced what "doing it right" looked like, or felt like. It hasn't been your fault if you have always felt that other people knew some secrets about successful relationships that you didn't know.

You may feel overwhelmingly guilty because you have been so ineffectual in your intimate relationships. Even if you learn nothing else from reading this book, please accept, right now, that you are not to blame for the pain you have suffered—and inflicted—to this point.

You didn't have an effective role model for loving relationships. You have had to make it all up. What you *did* know is that you didn't want to be like your parents, but you didn't know how to filter the destructive actions from the good actions. So you created a fantasy about how ideal relationships work from a fanciful blend of what you imagined, saw at a distance or observed on TV.

All of us learned to relate to others by watching how our parents interacted with each other, and with their children. Take a minute before you read further to create a visual picture for yourself of the interactions you observed between your parents. Think how you related to your mother, to your father. Do not judge. Just look objectively at your childhood experiences as you re-member them. Your relationship behavior as an adult, no matter how different it may look, is, in large measure, a reaction to those experiences.

You will learn better ways to interact with others as you read this book. You will have new options and choices. And you will have a new responsibility to choose the better ways.

I want you to picture the model for your adult relationships which you learned while you were growing up in an alcoholic family. The following pages, originally published as an article in *Focus* magazine, will give you a broad overview. Think about your own childhood and your own family as you read it.

CHEMICAL DEPENDENCY: THE INSIDIOUS INVADER

Where did it go wrong? What happened? Who is responsible? Where is the sense? What does it mean? Where will it all end? Circles and circles of circles and circles—all filled with confusion. Where did we go off the track? Is it possible to understand?

For each couple, the beginning is different. Even so, the process that occurs in the chemically dependent marital relationship is essentially the same. For the starting point, let's take a look at the marriage vows. Most wedding services include the following statements: for better or worse—for richer or poorer—in sickness and in health—until death do us part. Maybe that's where the trouble began. Did you mean what you said when you said it? If you knew at that time that you were going to have not the better but the worse, not the health but the sickness, not the richer but the poorer, and the potential suicide, would the love that you felt have made it worth it? You may say so, but I wonder. If you were more realistic than romantic, you may have interpreted the vows to mean: through the bad as well as the good, assuming that the bad times would be transitory, and the good ones permanent. The contract is entered into in good faith. There is no benefit of hindsight.

The idealizing that takes place at this time is not realistic. This is true not only for those who will live with chemical dependence, but for everyone. The difference is that the reality continues to be distorted in the chemically dependent relationship, and little by little the couple loses touch with what a happy marital relationship is all about. If the statistics are accurate, and they probably are understated, then a very large percentage of you grew up in chemically dependent households. This is important to be aware of, because you probably had no idea how to develop a healthy marital relationship to begin with. Your early attempts to "do it right" were built on models that you had not seen nor experienced, but rather made up in your own head. Thus, the fancifulness of the vows would play right into this notion of "It will be different for us."

By the time help is sought, the expectations have changed a great deal. The sense of self is gone for the chemically free partner. "How can I help him/her?" The sense of what one can expect in a relationship has shifted. It is no longer Camelot. It is no longer even person-to-person. The distortion is bizarre. I will stay because "He doesn't beat me." "She doesn't run around." "He hasn't lost his job." Imagine getting credit for the behaviors we ordinary mortals do as a matter of course. Even if the worst is true—even if he does beat you—even if she does run around—even if he is no longer working. Even with all this, you will then say, "But I love him/her!" When I respond, "Tell me, what is so lovable?" there is no response. The answer doesn't come, but the power of being emotionally stuck is far greater than the power of reason. I know it, but I plant the seed regardless.

Somewhere between the vows of everlasting wonderfulness, and the acceptance of life as a horror story, lies the reality. Somewhere hidden in the muck is the truth. It didn't get distorted overnight. It started out on one end of the pendulum and landed on the other. Somehow the process was so gradual that no one saw it happening, and the middle ground went unnoticed.

If I ask, "What *was* lovable when you decided to

marry?" the response comes quickly. It is not unusual to hear answers like, "There was a strong physical attraction, and we could talk about anything and everything. He/she was my lover and my best friend."

These sentiments are sincere and important. It is important to recognize that people who start out as friends and lovers have something special. It is important, therefore, to recognize that chemical dependency affects everything. It turns lovers and friends into adversaries. Friendship is based on a number of things. It is based on mutual trust and honesty. It is based on the ability to communicate openly. It is based on a sense of understanding and being understood. The chemical eats away at this slowly, but surely.

The erosion probably begins in the denial phase. At this stage, the drinking is causing problems, but no one wants to face up to it. So the lies begin. First the lies to the self, and then the lies to each other. The dependent person will lie mostly in terms of broken promises. The chemically free person will lie to cover up. The trust begins to break down. True feelings are held back until they become explosive. The honest communication begins to dissolve.

The physical relationship is a good indicator of what is happening in the total relationship. The attraction may well continue through the denial phase. It will continue to be a way of sharing, even as the words become more difficult. Not only that, but no one has yet to come up with a better way of making up after a drunken episode.

Gradually, the interest in physical intimacy will decline on the part of the chemically free partner. The need to be less vulnerable will start to take over. At this point, the sexual experience may still be technically satisfying, but the emotion is held in check.

As in all other aspects, the deterioration continues, and what was a warm, loving experience now becomes a power play and a means of ventilating anger.

"Go to bed with your bottle—not me!" "I can't stand the smell!" "You have to make a choice!" "Who needs you? It won't be hard to find someone better than you!"

The gap continues to get greater. No part of the relationship remains unaffected.

The climate becomes confused and the open communication that existed before gives way to suspicion and anger. The underlying concerns are not addressed and the couple, even though they still care about each other, live a distorted lifestyle. Both partners are being directed by the chemical—one directly, the other indirectly. One is addicted to the chemical; the other is addicted to the chemically dependent partner.

The relationship breaks down even further. . . . If the chemical dependency was only destructive to this point, the damage to the relationship is repairable. It is possible to argue it out and, at the very least, clear the air. Feelings can be expressed and the lines of communication can remain open. But this is not simple.

This insidious illness does not stop here. It separates the couple still further. The chemically dependent partner stops developing emotionally. The chemically dependent partner no longer wants to deal with or confront problems. A large part of any marital relationship involves making decisions and resolving shared problems. Where will we go on our vacation? Johnny is failing algebra again. Can we redo the kitchen?

And so on, with the stuff that life is made of. These issues are no longer shared. The chemically free partner takes over more and more responsibility. The resentment grows deeper. The gap becomes even greater.

A saving grace during difficult times is the support of caring family and friends. This is true here, too, at least for a while, but if they have not experienced what you are experiencing, the support will only increase the pain. If only they could understand. The isolation of the chemically dependent couple becomes greater. They become isolated from other people, and they grow further and further away from each other.

And the sickness continues. The feelings shared are similar. The pain and the desperation are felt by both, but they blame each other. The guilt is felt by both, but the responsibility is placed differently. Once close, you are now strangers most of the time.

Occasionally, you will find yourselves in the eye of the storm, and you will be so grateful. The idea is that now the drinking will stop and all will be as it was. It is a shared belief. It is a shared deception. The reality is that the disease will progress. It will get worse . . . and so will whatever is left of your relationship.

The communication deteriorates into forms of anger. The inner feelings evolve into worry, fear, despair. The feelings are shared, but in isolation. The chemically dependent partner numbs the feelings, and the nonabuser is doubled over in pain—relieved only by anger and occasional fantasies.

The fantasy is that the drinking will stop, and everything will be as it was in the beginning. The miracle of abstinence. The fantasy is shared. Alcohol will lose its hold, and you will live happily ever after.

Somehow that is the greatest lie of all, and yet one of the most universally believed. The drinking stops. What does that mean in terms of the relationship? It only means that the focus is lost. It only means that the chemical is no longer the focal point. A huge vacuum now exists. Nothing else happens automatically. The trust that was lost does not come back just because the abuse stops. Just as a history of unfulfilled promises damaged the trust, a new history has to come into play, in order to rebuild it. The lies may stop, but sharing makes one too vulnerable to be open at this point. The anger does not automatically go away because the drinking stops. The feelings that were repressed by the chemical may want to come cascading out. How terribly insecure—how terribly frightening. How hard to share these feelings and expect to be understood. The lines of communication have been cut off. You are two blind people without a road map.

Abstinence is not enough. A whole new relationship has to be built. The new starting point has to be different from the original starting point. The starting point this time is best served in learning how to solve mutual problems. It is best served in developing guidelines of how to talk to and not at each other. How can each be heard and understood? If the relationship is going to be healthy, it is going to require a lot of hard work. The foundation will require careful and long attention. The attraction that enhances the beginning of a relationship is no longer present. The basis now has to be firmly grounded in reality. If both parties are committed to working, it can be more than it would have been, had the chemical not entered into the picture. If both people are looking for the same things, there is a great opportunity for mutual, as well as individual, growth. If not, the fantasy is over. The relationship is done. Abstinence is not nirvana.

Chemical dependency destroys slowly, but thoroughly. Chemical independence can lead the way to build a healthy marital relationship. It's the only winning game in town.

Who Do You Pick
for Your Lover?

Why Do You Pick the Lovers That You Do?

Everything is going wrong with my relationship. I know that it's all my fault. I try everything I know to fix it, but it doesn't work. I'm not even sure if I love him/her. Maybe I don't know what love is. I'm so confused."

Sound familiar? It should. It is almost verbatim the story I hear when an Adult Child of an Alcoholic enters therapy because an intimate relationship is souring. And the story is the same whether the COA is twenty years old and in a first serious relationship, or forty years old and the veteran of one or more failed marriages.

"It just has to be my fault. Relationships always go this way. I thought it would be different this time, but it wasn't. Maybe I'm better off alone."

Have you felt that way? We all have—and we've all said similar self-deprecating things while in the midst of a troubled or troublesome relationship. Is it a "normal" way to feel? It depends upon whether you are feeling that way because of the current circumstances or whether these are deep-seated messages which have become a permanent part of your self-image because they were hammered at you time and time again while you were growing up. In both cases, the feelings are equally painful, but they are more difficult to erase in the second case.

Read those opening statements again: "Everything is going wrong. I know that it is all my fault. I try to do everything that I know, but it just doesn't work."

Today you are saying those phrases about your relationship. The context may be new for you, but the phrases and the feelings are not. Once again, you are experiencing the helplessness of your childhood and reacting to an "old tape." Nonetheless, the feelings are real, and, oh, so powerful.

Other familiar feelings also well up, including confusion, the sense of being stuck, of being unable to change your destiny.

This is all part of being in an intimate relationship. It will drag out all things, old and new, that you have experienced and felt before. You will play it all out again. With work, the process and outcomes will be different, but the struggle cannot be avoided. Even those who have not been affected by living in an alcoholic family find one must work to have a good and healthy relationship. You have plenty of company in the struggle!

To probe a little deeper into the nature of the struggle you are facing, it is important that you recall some of the early inconsistent messages you were given by your parents. Like it or not, want to believe it or not, these messages are still influencing you on an unconscious level throughout all aspects of your life. *To change your life, you must change the message.*

And, awareness is the first step toward changing the message. The knowledge of how your current patterns were formed will begin to release you from the self-critical indictment which is such a basic part of your nature. Let's take a look at these double-bind messages and how they affect you today:

"I love you. Go away."

Sometimes your alcoholic parent was warm and loving, sometimes rejecting and hostile. Although your non-alcoholic parent told you that you were loved, he or she was often so absorbed with worry and so irritable that you rarely felt loved. There was no consistency.

This is love as you understood it as a child, and are still experiencing it. Ever wonder why you are attracted to that person who is warm and loving one day, and reject-ing the next? Ever wonder why the person who says he or she will call and doesn't seems more desirable than the one who is consistent?

If, by chance, you do become involved with a lover who is consistent, you find that sort of person very unset-tling, because you have no frame of reference for this kind of behavior. I am talking about the type of indi-vidual with order in his/her life, the person who can pre-dict with a reasonable amount of certainty what tomorrow will bring. This also is someone who will behave, feel and think tomorrow much as he/she behaved, felt and thought today. The challenge to win the love of the erratic and sometimes rejecting person repeats the challenge of your childhood. You are grateful when the inconsistent person throws you a crumb, but get bored quickly with the one who is available all the time.

You are playing out your childhood all over again, because the only consistency you knew was inconsis-tency. The only predictability you had was the lack of predictability. You lived your childhood on an emotional roller coaster. And that is what you understand. Think a minute: How many times have you created a crisis in your relationship to get the energy flowing again, and bring the relationship back to more familiar ground?

Even though this may be obvious to you on an intellectual level, bear in mind that it may take longer for you to truly feel this truth because you were conditioned at such an early age.

"You can't do anything right. I need you."

Here is another set of conflicting messages which you play over and over again. When you were a child, you could never meet your alcoholic parent's perfectionistic standards, no matter how hard you tried. You were never good enough. And you truly believed that everything that went wrong was your fault. If you would have been good enough, things would have been better for your family.

Yet you knew you were needed, and that they couldn't get along without you. That was perfectly clear also. Since it was impossible for them to get along without you, even though you were so worthless, you would struggle until you could find a way to "fix" things.

As an adult, do you find yourself drawn to partners
who are both extremely dependent and highly critical?
Are you drawn to those who repeatedly put you down,
although you know they can't get along without you?
You continue to strive for their approval, because on a
deep level you believe that there would not be so much
trouble in the relationship if you were only good enough.
And you know you can't keep letting down someone
who needs you so desperately. Sound familiar? Another
setup.

**"Yes, it's true that your mother/father did/said
those terrible things. But you must understand
that he/she was drunk."**

The implications of this double-bind message are especially destructive to you when you are in an intimate
relationship. Your unconscious tells you that if you can
find an explanation for inexcusable behavior, you must
believe that the behavior is excusable.

In the family system affected by alcoholism, the alcoholic is rarely held accountable for his/her behavior.
More likely, the child hears from the other parent,
"What did you expect from a drunk?" Or, in early family
recovery, "You have to understand that your

father/mother has a disease." The child hears the message that the parent can do whatever he or she wishes by simply using the excuse of drunkenness or alcoholism.

Now that you are an adult, you have become the most understanding person in the world when it comes to your loving relationships. Right? In almost every situation, you will find a way to make everything okay—certainly if *someone* must be at fault, you will take that fault upon yourself. You have learned how to understand, and you have learned how to take full responsibility upon yourself.

Therefore, when you are treated in a lousy way, you analyze the situation and don't allow yourself to experience any angry feelings. Understanding a behavior does not make it automatically acceptable. But you learned to do that very well when you were a child, and denied yourself the pain for maltreatment because you believed that "My father/mother wouldn't have done that to me if he/she were sober."

This also has elements of control and elements of guilt. Here is the kind of thought pattern that runs through the mind of the child in the alcoholic family system: "If I feel guilty, then I am responsible. And if I am responsible, then I can do something to fix it, to change it, to make it different." Giving up your guilt also means giving up your sense that you have control over the situation. And, of course, loss of control is a disaster. You have grown up to be the perfect doormat for an inconsiderate person. Often you end up in a perfect give-and-take relationship . . . you give, they take.

"I'll be there for you—next time. I give you my word."

The underlying message here is—forget it! So you learn how not to want so that you don't get disappointed.

Sometimes you unwittingly become the doormat for a partner who truly doesn't want to treat you that way. Often you become tired and resentful. You complain about having to do everything in the relationship—yet it is almost impossible for you to ask for anything for yourself. You want your partner to be a mind reader.

Your fear of asking for something and then not getting it is as unsettling as your fear of asking for something *and* getting it! The first outcome reinforces your belief that you are too unworthy to deserve what you want, and the second possibility is so unfamiliar that you actually don't know how to react. Even a simple compliment may cause you great discomfort.

You deal with the whole situation by abdicating

responsibility for your happiness. You decide that your partner should know what you want and act on it without ever having been told. For example, "If I have to tell him I want to go to the theater for my birthday, it proves that he doesn't really want to please me." Your lover is now set up so that you can decide he doesn't love you if he doesn't pick up whatever vague hints you may have sent his way. You'll only be happy with a mind reader, a fantasy hero who will automatically know how to please you.

"Everything is fine, so don't worry. But how in the world can I deal with all this?"

Both of these messages come through. "Don't concern yourself—everything is going to be okay." Yet the underlying sense you get from your parents is that everything is *not* okay. The result is you develop into a superperson by the time you become an adult. You can (and will) take care of everything. You are in charge. Nobody else around you has to be concerned about anything. You can manage. How often do you say the following things: "Don't worry, we'll take my car—I've got enough money—I'll pick up the food—I'll make the arrangements—Don't worry—It's no problem for me!"

What Is a Healthy
Relationship Anyway?

What does a healthy relationship look like? What does it feel like? How do I get one? How will I know if I have one?"

These are very important and real questions that need to be addressed. Wanting to be involved in a healthy, intimate relationship is a universal condition. And defining just exactly what "healthy" is, is a universal question.

You know you are in a healthy, intimate relationship when you have created an environment where:

1. I can be me.
2. You can be you.
3. We can be us.

4. I can grow.
5. You can grow.
6. We can grow together.

Essentially, that's what it's all about. It's paradoxical that a healthy relationship frees me to be myself—and yet I don't know who I am because acquiring self-knowledge is a lifelong process. Although you may not have a strong sense of who you are, you recognize clearly when you are *not* being allowed the freedom to be you. It is clear when you are feeling judged. It is clear when you feel that you are walking on eggshells. It is clear when you worry about making a mistake. In effect, the freedom to be you means that your partner will not interfere with nor judge your process of being and becoming.

You offer your partner the same freedom that you are asking for yourself. And you accept your partner as he/she is, and do not try to use the power of your love to turn him/her into a swan. You do not get caught up in your fantasy of who you want him or her to be, and then concentrate on making that happen. You focus on who that person really is.

"I accept you unconditionally, and you accept me unconditionally." That's the bottom line. It does not mean that changes in personality or actions are undesirable or impossible—it merely means that you begin by accepting your partner as he or she is.

"We are free to be us." Each couple defines their own relationship built on shared values and interests. First, they must decide what they each value as individuals and then they can build a oneness out of their separateness.

Some of their differences are unimportant, and can either be ignored or worked out. For example, issues such as "You always leave the cap off the toothpaste," or, "I hate church socials," can easily be worked out.

Other differences are significant and need to be worked out, if the relationship is to remain healthy and survive. Examples of more critical issues are, "I don't want any children," or, "I'll never have anything to do with your mother again."

Many experiences are enhanced because the two of you are a couple. Enjoying together the beauty of a sunset, a walk on the beach, a well-prepared meal, are examples of the "us" that make a partnership desirable. "I am enhanced when I have me—you have you—and we also have us."

A healthy relationship creates an environment where you can grow. In this climate of support, you also encourage your partner to do the same. Through the directions of your individual growth, you develop together as a couple.

A couple also grows together by developing mutual goals and working together on ways to achieve them. Interestingly, it is the journey toward the goals, and not necessarily the goals themselves, which help the relationship grow. Whether or not you attain a goal is part of the process toward the next shared experience.

Intimacy means that you have a love relationship with another person where you offer, and are offered, validation, understanding, and a sense of being valued intellectually, emotionally and physically.

The more you are willing to share, and be shared with, the greater the degree of intimacy.

A healthy relationship is not a power struggle. The two of you don't have to think the same way about all things.

A healthy relationship is not symbiotic. You do not have to feel the same way about all things.

A healthy relationship is not confined to a sexual relationship which must end in orgasm, but celebrates the sharing and exploring.

Relationship Issues
Shared by Adult
Children of Alcoholics

You have been living with many myths generated and perpetuated by your family system. Because of this, you put such enormous pressure on yourself that you wonder whether having a healthy, intimate relationship is worth paying the price.

You are torn apart by push-pull issues which may be illusionary to others, but are very real, and sometimes paralyzing, to you.

"I want to become involved. I don't want to become involved."

"I want to meet someone. I don't want to meet someone."

"I want to get to know you better. Please, simply go away."

These issues interfere with your ability to get what you want out of relationships.

Your first step is to take a good, hard look at these myths. Acknowledge them. Reject them. Then replace them with what exists in the real world. This is by no means a small task, because you have been living with these myths for a long time. They will not vanish overnight. Simply becoming aware of them is the place to begin.

COA MYTH

"If I am involved with you, I will lose me."

TRUTH: In the real world, healthy relationships enhance the self and do not absorb it.

Fear of Loss of Self

This fear is present because you never clearly established your sense of self while you were growing into adulthood. The early messages that you received from your parents were very confusing. The lack of clear messages forced you to create many of your beliefs and values, rather than learning them through example.

Because your parents didn't consistently care for you in all the ways that a child needs care, you have had to do a lot of self-parenting. This has left you with an inconclusive sense of who you really are. Your selfhood is still in the state of evolving and is easily influenced. Ideally, by the time one reaches adulthood, the inner messages are much stronger than the outside influences. In other words, your decision-making evolves out of what your knowledge and instincts tell you, rather than depending upon what you are reading or being told at the moment.

For COAs, this state of confidence in your ability to make decisions and act upon them is not reached so easily. Someone (anyone) else's opinion often influences yours. So, if you have been working on being your own person, and having confidence in your decision-making skills, you may feel threatened by the idea of involvement with another person whose opinions and ideas will be important to you—and may influence you in ways you don't want.

Feeling this sense of insecurity does not automatically mean the "loss of self." What it does mean is that you will "check out" many of your perceptions, opinions and responses more carefully, to see where they are coming from. This provides valuable information for you. Your next step is to not automatically dismiss your opinions in favor of new input. Think it over. Give yourself a little time to assess and consider the situation.

This gives you three choices in every situation: You may maintain your original position, change your position, or adopt an entirely new position which incorporates both your thinking on the subject and that of others. You will feel much more confident about the decisions that you make, and less threatened by other people's opinions.

COA MYTH

"If you really knew me, you wouldn't care about me."

TRUTH: You probably aren't as good an actor or actress as you think you are. Your beloved probably *already* really knows you. And cares about you anyway!

Fear of Being Found Out

Many COAs constantly worry that the person they love would want nothing more to do with them if he or she really knew them. Although it's a little vague to you about just who that real and horrendous person may be, you still feel the anxious feelings very strongly.

You try to stave off this possibility by acting out your

fantasies of how a perfect person would act. You try to behave as though you have your entire life in order and are totally problem-free. After all, the simply human, real you with human frailties will never be good enough for someone you love.

This belief is not something you made up. Since childhood, you have been told overtly and covertly that you are the cause of family difficulties. Getting close to a loved one will expose your dark side and cause that person to negate the positive side of you that they have loved until now.

Changing this belief as an adult begins with hard, cold logic. Think about it. Were you really powerful enough as a child to cause your family problems? Truthfully, you will have to answer "no."

COA MYTH

"If you find out that I am not perfect, you will abandon me."

TRUTH: Nobody is perfect. And perfection does not exist.

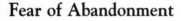

Fear of Abandonment

Fear of abandonment is very strong in COAs and differs from the fear of rejection. Adult Children of Alcoholics seem to be able to handle rejection and adjust to it. Fear of abandonment, however, cuts a lot deeper because of childhood experiences.

The child who experiences living with alcoholism grows into an individual with a weak and very inconsistent sense of self, as we have already discussed. This is a very, very critical self which has not had the nurturance it needed. It is a hungry self and, in many ways, a very insecure self.

This is caused by the fact that you never knew when, or if, your parents would be emotionally available to you. You expected unpredictability and inconsistency. Once the drinking began, you simply did not exist. Your needs would not be met until the drinking episode and any accompanying crises were over. There was no way to predict when this would occur. What a terrible, terrible feeling. No matter what you did to try to prevent it, it would happen anyway.

Some children living in this situation continue trying to get their needs met, and others give up entirely. Those children who give up entirely are not as anxious to enter into adult relationships as are those who still hold onto the fantasy that maybe, just maybe, this time things will be different.

The constant fear, however, is that the person you love will not be there for you tomorrow. In an attempt to guard against losing your beloved, you idealize the relationship and idealize your role in the relationship. Your safeguard against being abandoned is to try hard to be perfect and serve all the other person's needs.

Whenever anything goes wrong (and in life, things go wrong), and when there is conflict (and in life, there is conflict), the fear of being abandoned takes precedence over dealing with the pertinent issue which needs to be resolved. This fear is so great that it is not unusual for COAs to completely lose sight of the actual problem.

A typical example of this is illustrated by the argument that Mary A., aged 26 (one of six children whose father is still actively drinking), had with her boyfriend. It erupted because he was paying attention to other women, and Mary got angry. The boyfriend responded defensively, told her that she was being paranoid, and the argument continued.

When he left, Mary's anger soon turned into a sense of panic.

"Oh, my God! I'm sure I was wrong. Maybe I was

overreacting. Maybe he doesn't care about me anymore. Maybe he's going to leave me now. After all, if I weren't so insecure, his behavior wouldn't have bothered me." It was a classic example of feeling abandoned.

Within three hours, Mary A. drove to her boyfriend's home, gave him a red rose and apologized for *her* behavior. He accepted her apology, and they made love.

As she was recounting the story to me later, I asked her, "How did you resolve the issue?"

She looked puzzled at first, and then said, "Oh, that!"

Her terrible fear of abandonment had erased the issue from her mind. The problem itself was lost when the panic set in. Reducing the pain of her fear of abandonment became her primary goal.

In cases like this, the problem doesn't go away just because it is being ignored. It will recur—maybe in the same form and maybe in a different form—until it is dealt with, or until it becomes a significant underlying issue with the couple. Repressing the problem does not cause it to be truly forgotten.

Mary's problem also illustrates the fears of "loss of self" and "being found out."

Mary starts placing all her emphasis on his reaction to the experience. Then she begins to wonder and worry about his reaction to other experiences. She thinks about him constantly, particularly at times when he is not being attentive to her. She focuses entirely on him, what he thinks of her, and how she can keep from losing him.

What about Mary's needs? What about the fact she simply did not want to experience the way he was ignoring her to flirt with other women? She starts judging herself harshly for reacting to his behavior. And the woman who felt that reaction begins to disappear, something Mary recognizes and hates in herself. The next time I saw Mary she commented, "I tend to lose myself in every relationship when I am involved. Maybe I should end it now."

Mary does not believe she is worth very much, and is fearful he will discover that. She believes she can fool him, if she is on her best behavior. This creates heavy tension in the relationship, but she is afraid to be open and honest. Now she begins to wonder whether she reacted appropriately, and says, "This is really my fault. If I were more secure, I wouldn't have been so upset when he paid attention to other women. My insecurities are getting in the way.

"If he knows how insecure I really am, he may not bother with me anymore. Perhaps it is just as well that we ended the argument the way we did. I want him to see me as a 'together' woman, not as a scared little girl. He wouldn't have anything to do with that scared little girl."

How long can Mary pretend to be somebody else? The truth of the matter is that he probably already sees the "scared little girl" aspects of her personality, and is attracted to the whole complex person that she is. She probably doesn't hide her fears as well as she thinks she does—or would like to!

It isn't important whether Mary reacted to her boyfriend's behavior because of her own insecurities, or because he was being somewhat obnoxious. It probably is a combination of both. What is important is that the couple can discuss the issue.

If she is insecure, she won't become more secure by denying these feelings. She needs to acknowledge these feelings, and then have the relationship develop to the point where she feels more secure. If he cares about her the way he says he does, he will attempt to accommodate her feelings. It is just as important for her to recognize if he is not interested in accommodating her feelings and prefers to play. Lack of accommodation on a relatively minor issue may signal lack of accommodation on more significant issues which will arise in the future. If this is the case, this relationship may not offer Mary what she is seeking.

COA MYTH
"We are as one."

TRUTH: In the real world, you are you, and I am me. And then there is us.

Bonding

Chances are that you did not experience the bonding in your early years that children in more typical homes did, especially if your mother was the alcoholic. You could not depend on your parents taking care of your needs in a consistent way. You could not depend on being held and loved to solve your fears and calm your hurts. You could not trust that your mother would nurture you when you felt badly, whether you were right or wrong.

This affects the way you become involved, and the intensity of that involvement today.

Chris L., aged 33, whose mother is an alcoholic, was taking a course in group dynamics at a local college. She reported that she didn't fit in with her classmates because they were concerned with their struggle to *break* the bonds with their parents, while her lifelong struggle was in trying to *develop* bonds.

It is important to understand the difference and recognize the implications for the early stages of a relationship. Adults who had many of their needs satis-fied at home (many to an unhealthy degree!) are able to let an involvement develop slowly. The investment can take place slowly, along with the growth of trust.

Those who are products of homes where bonding never took place, if they invest at all, invest at once, heavily and on a deep emotional level. They seize the opportunity for bonding and are deeply involved before they know what is happening.

In the early stages of a relationship, there is great intensity of feelings. The body chemistry that attracts you to each other is activated, and both parties are super-attentive and super-involved. You understand this degree of intensity because it feels to you like the energizing you experience in a crisis.

This is the time when both parties greatly desire fusion. You are on each other's minds all the time—the phone calls are frequent—the desire to be together is great. Emotionally, it is a very powerful time.

The early stages are probably more an "involvement" than a "relationship." It is the playing out of a fantasy. You cannot sustain this intensity which is so appealing. This is just a dynamite beginning, and not what a healthy relationship is all about.

Initially, this is flattering to the new partner, and the

closeness feels good. Often, the partner gets pleasure out of feeling needed and in fulfilling the needs of the love object. But after a while this begins to feel suffocating, and starts to become a drain. Your partner, if healthy, will stop wanting to be devoted completely and exclusively to the relationship. Life holds other priorities, as well. The aura of the ideal love evaporates as a result, and things begin to be put into perspective.

When life begins to normalize, the intensity decreases. The telephone quits ringing all the time, and you feel let down and rejected. You feel that your partner no longer cares because he/she no longer desires to spend every moment with you. From your point of view, this feels like abandonment. It's the drunk versus sober parent scenario once again. You feel the gaping hole inside you even more deeply than before.

Clutching at your partner will force him/her into the "I love you, go away" stance, even though your beloved still cares. If you continue to play out your script, you will set yourself up for what you fear the most: rejection and abandonment. Then you will feel very confused because all you wanted was a loving relationship, and you will think once again you picked the wrong person. The truth may be that you were asking unrealistic things of your relationship. It is important that you be very clear about what you want your relationship to fulfill within you so that you avoid this situation.

On the other hand, you may react by deciding you no longer care, and leaving the budding relationship. This may mean you are "hooked" on intensity, and have fooled yourself into equating intensity with the relationship itself. Or, it may mean that you are terrified about beginning the process of getting to know and being known by another person. It probably is a little of both.

COA MYTH

"Being vulnerable always has negative results."

TRUTH: In the real world, being vulnerable sometimes has negative results and sometimes has positive results. But it is the only route to intimacy.

Vulnerability

Early on you learned that you were the only one who could be responsible for your happiness, and that other people could make you angry only if you permitted it. You learned that you were in charge of your feelings. This was essential and critical to your being able to survive emotionally in an alcoholic household. But now you need to open up your feelings to others if you want to participate in a healthy, intimate relationship.

It seems to me that the *idea* of being vulnerable is really more terrifying than actually *being* vulnerable. This was underlined for me by the discussions which took place one Monday night in one of our ACOA group meetings. Jimmy opened it up by telling how intensely sharing his feelings in the previous group meeting had affected him all week. "I left feeling so vulnerable," he said, "and the vulnerability lasted all week. I tried to be alone most of the time, because I was afraid of what would happen if I were with others while I felt so open to devastation."

The other group members understood what he was saying and agreed with him.

"Hey, wait a minute!" I said. "What does being vulnerable mean to you people? And what are you talking about when you say that you are afraid to be vulnerable?"

One by one, every person there defined "allowing themselves to be vulnerable" as being out of control of their lives. They felt that someone else would then take control of their lives and do them damage. To them, there seemed to be no other way. Vulnerability meant loss of self, devastation, being powerless to prevent these negative things from happening.

"When I was a child," Malone shared, "I was afraid that I would be killed if I let my guard down for even one minute." Allowing vulnerability, to her, meant potential death. Although it didn't mean the possibility of death to the others, it did mean something terrible. It represented being left out, being hurt.

Just talking about feeling vulnerable created a very tense and somewhat depressing climate within the group.

"This is a very important thing for us to examine," I said. "If we are to develop healthy intimate relationships, we must allow our partner access to our feelings. There is no other way to do it. If you are too terrified of being vulnerable and its consequences to take a risk, you are automatically saying that you are incapable or unwilling to have a healthy, intimate relationship.

"Have you ever considered the possibility that many of the feelings you are defending against are feelings which would actually enhance your life? Have you considered the fact that there are many aspects of love feelings that you haven't felt? That there are feelings of excitement about being in your presence that you don't feel? That there are supportive feelings that you don't allow yourself to feel? Have you considered that there is a whole spectrum of feelings you have denied yourself because your terror about being vulnerable takes control of your life?"

Leslie shared that after three years, she is able to be emotionally accessible to the man she loves. "I no longer have any secrets, emotional or otherwise," she said. "I tore down my walls little by little. Sometimes I've rebuilt a piece of them because I became afraid or because he didn't react the way I had hoped he would. But, slowly and gradually, I was able to let down the barriers as our relationship grew and our trust developed.

"I don't know many others whom I would trust in this way, but I do know that it has not been harmful to me to be vulnerable in this relationship. It has, in effect, made me stronger. Once I really allowed him into my life, he could begin helping me feel things about myself which had been a struggle to feel before. And that helps me feel more solid, more secure as a person.

"It hasn't been easy, but it has been worth the struggle!"

This reinforced for the group that the idea of being vulnerable may be more terrifying than the actual experience. In reality, you wouldn't even be reading this book if you were not interested in personal growth. Growth does not take place unless we allow access to new thoughts, feelings and ideas. And this access is gained only by being open to it, which means allowing ourselves to be vulnerable.

COA MYTH

"We will never argue or criticize each other."

TRUTH: In the real world, couples argue from time to time, and are critical of each other's behavior.

Anger

Adult Children of Alcoholics believe that in an ideal relationship there will be no conflict and no anger. Although they recognize intellectually that this is impossible, emotionally this is what they want. Anger is very complicated and very much misunderstood by them. Historically, anger needed to be repressed. Children growing up with alcoholism live in a very angry climate, where it is never resolved. Expressing anger is never useful and only tends to make life worse. It never did anyone any good.

Therefore, COAs learn how not to be angry. Instead they rationalize, explain things away and finally become depressed. The words they use to describe their depression are words of anger. Since anger is repressed, the only time it comes out is when it is no longer containable and has turned into rage. Rage is frightening to COAs because they don't know what they might do. It is not unusual for one to say, "I am terrified of allowing myself to be angry because if I lose control of my anger, I might kill." Many turn this anger inward, and since they would never harm others, have suicidal thoughts.

They also fear another person's anger being expressed toward them. Anger may cause physical violence, which must be avoided at all costs. This is another submerged issue which comes into play in a relationship. Yet, there is no way to have a good relationship without resolving conflict. If two people are healthy and alive, and have thoughts and ideas, there will be times when they disagree. There will also be times when one person does something that irritates the other and makes him/her angry. It is impossible to know in a developing relationship where all the sensitive spots are. The ideal is to talk it over when anger surfaces, learn where it comes from, and how not to repeat it.

ACOAs often translate anger into something that it is not. It goes something like this: "If I am angry with you, I don't love you. If you are angry with me, you don't love me. Since I do love you, then I can't allow myself to be angry at you. If you really love me, you will not be angry at me either." On an emotional level, this is the message that the Adult Child gives to himself. Though not a valid message, it plays out just the same: "If I cannot contain my anger at you, I must reject you. If you do not contain your anger at me, then you must reject me." Once again, the issue that made the couple angry has been forgotten. Why even bother to deal with it if the outcome will be rejection?

In addition, because Adult Children have no experience in problem-solving with another person, they don't know how to resolve the angry feelings. They don't know how to work with their anger in order to dissipate it. Anger needs to be expressed, in one way or another. It needs to be recognized, acknowledged, talked over, understood and dissipated. It is important to realize that anger is an ever-present, hidden issue in the relationships of ACOAs.

Part of what made Mary believe her boyfriend was going to abandon her, or that she had to reject him, was her anger. Since she did not understand how to resolve anger, these were the only alternatives she saw.

In addition to being terrified at the depth of their anger, COAs are also uncertain about its appropriateness. "Would that make a normal person angry?" is the question I often hear. It is asked in reference to both their own anger and that of the people with whom they are involved. "Just what is okay to be angry about?" they want to know. Recently, I gave a lecture on COAs which a client and her boyfriend attended. He said, "I came because I want to know as much as I can about the things that have affected Carol, because I love her." I was most impressed.

They sat on the right side of the room, and most of the rest of the students sat on the left. About one-half hour into the lecture, a security guard walked into the room and turned out the light. I made a comment to him, and he turned it back on and left the room. I made light of my annoyance and went on with the lecture. The next time I saw Carol, she told me how furious Bill had become. "How could anyone walk into a room, look directly at you and turn out the light? The discourtesy was outrageous!" She said, "You know, it didn't bother me at all. I guess I'm used to being treated as if I don't exist."

For them, Bill's anger was an important learning experience. It was clear to her that she needed to work on her own self-worth. And he learned how deep the lack of validation is for COAs. Asking the question about whether the reaction was "normal" prompted the insight. Who is to say what is normal? You react according to your history, and when your reactions are put into perspective, you decide what is normal.

COA MYTH

"Anything that goes wrong is my fault. I am a terrible person."

TRUTH: In the real world, some things that go wrong are your fault. Some things are not. Terrible things happen, but you are not terrible.

Guilt and Shame

Guilt and shame emerge in any relationship with someone who has grown up with alcoholism. They are issues which need to be worked on. Ernie Kurtz, in his booklet, *Shame and Guilt: Characteristics of the Dependency Cycle*, describes guilt as "a feeling of wrong-doing, sense of wickedness, 'not good.'" The child is taught that what goes wrong is his fault. Even if it wasn't his fault, he hears, "If you were not such a rotten kid, I would not have to drink." The guilt that many COAs have is on a level so deep that they believe that their very existence caused the problem.

Shame, although somewhat different, is very closely linked to guilt, and one tends to feed off the other. Dr. Kurtz describes shame as "a feeling of inadequacy, sense of worthlessness, 'no good.'" Guilt is associated with behavior, while shame relates to the essence of the person, the self, which is even more basic to the person. It is very hard to overcome these feelings. It is a lifelong struggle to feel that your behavior is not "no good;" it is also a lifelong struggle to believe that *you* are not "no good."

In a relationship, anything that goes wrong becomes, to some degree, your fault. You feel it is your fault because the things you do are no good, and because you are no good. It is your fault, because in growing up it was the only means of control you had. If you were responsible for what happened, then you believed you could do something to change it. It was, of course, futile because you were not responsible; but the struggle to try made you feel that you were not completely out of control. In a relationship, if something occurs about which you feel responsible, you think you can do something to change it. You can apologize, or you can do something different. If you are guilty, then you can do something. If you are not guilty, then you are, because of your mind-set, in a very real sense, stuck.

The idea of saying to your partner, "Why don't we take a look at this, regardless of whether I'm at fault, or you're at fault? I'm okay, and you're okay, and you and I need to find out what's going wrong," does not enter your mind. Because, essentially, you do not believe that you are okay.

Even if what you did was okay, you don't realize it. Therefore, every interaction gets extremely complicated. Also, you do not want the person with whom you are involved to kind out how inadequate or worthless you are. This, in turn, creates a climate in which you are less than totally honest. It goes back to the fear of "being found out."

COA MYTH

"In order to be lovable, I must be happy all the time."

TRUTH: In the real world, sometimes people are happy, and sometimes they are not.

Depression

Many ACOAs are what we call "chronically depressed." This means that there is an edge of sadness about them. As I discussed earlier, it results, in part, from the anger they have turned inward upon themselves. It also has to do with the experience of loss.

The Adult Child never got to be a child. He did not have the experience of being spontaneous, foolish, child-like—of doing the things that children normally do. He did not have an opportunity to experience fun, or even to know what fun is. Although he knows what it is to be worthless or impulsive, the experience of having fun is something that, if experienced at all, was negligible. This causes a degree of sadness, which makes it harder to feel free and spontaneous in any relationship. This causes depression. The Adult Child will fight against depression, because he tries to be pleasant in an attempt to be "the perfect partner." But, for many, the feeling of depression is always present beneath the surface.

Loss is also a major issue with ACOAs. They have, in effect, lost their childhood, and therefore many of the experiences other children have. For them, any change involves a loss of what they had before. Change is difficult because, psychologically, change means anarchy. With the fear of abandonment comes the fear of loss, accompanied by the ever-present fear that the relationship will not last. Once again, then, loss will have to be experienced. This fear causes a tremendous conflict. "I know it won't last, so I wait for the bomb to drop, and I panic at having to experience the loss, so I hold on tight." This kind of behavior tends to drive the other person away, which sets the dreaded fears in motion. Unfortunately, the feelings are not discussed, so there is little opportunity to begin to solve them.

The typical attitude is: "So that you do not see the level of my pain and how close it is to the surface, I will put on a 'happy face.' The song from *The King and I* about whistling a happy tune is my way of life."

COA MYTH

"We will trust each other totally, automatically and all at once."

TRUTH: In the real world, trust builds slowly.

Trust

It is natural for children to trust others. From infancy, they trust that their needs will be met. If this early trust is denied, they die, as they are completely helpless, and depend on others for nurture and care. Trust is so natural to children that, even in a typical family, they must be taught when not to be trusting. Children must be taught not to go with strangers, that it is not safe to run into the street, nor to touch the stove. Children, in their naivete, want to love and trust all people and all things.

In a home that has been affected by alcoholism, the child's needs are not totally unmet, but they are inconsistently met. This means that trusting people will mean being hurt, and therefore that trust is inappropriate. It means that the child must learn how to take care of himself. In order to survive, the child learns how not to trust . . . that he can depend only on himself. If someone is trustworthy, it is the exception rather than the rule. When there is an expectation, it is most often met by frustration and disappointment. "Don't trust" is something that the child learns very early and very well. However, contrary to the child's nature, it is an adaptive response to a maladaptive situation.

The discussion here is about how to build a healthy relationship. A major element—a necessary prerequisite for a healthy relationship—is trust. Without it, the relationship cannot prosper; it simply will not develop and grow. Trust is not easy to accomplish, because you have to unlearn many negative responses and feelings. You have to go all the way back to your early childhood, and once again begin to trust.

In a group of Adult Children, one young man said, "I have just started a new job. I like everyone I have met so far, but I am not going to trust anybody just yet. They are going to have to earn my trust." The group agreed with him. I said, "Why not trust everyone and then discount those who violate your trust? It will take much less energy. It doesn't mean you have to act in any particular way. If you decide to trust, you don't have to behave any differently than if you decided not to trust. It would just make it easier for you."

The group was fascinated and wanted to learn more about this approach, which was a new one for them. "It costs you nothing to trust automatically," I said. "You end up at the very same place. If you don't trust, and someone behaves in a manner that is untrustworthy, then you have affirmed and reinforced the fact that you can't trust anybody. If you do trust someone and he turns out not to be worthy of it, yes, you will be disappointed, but you will not be devastated. Disappointment is something that you have learned to handle very well. Affirming the fact that it was a good idea not to trust in the first place does not mean you will not be disappointed. That is the reality of it." This was a very curious idea to them—something that, given their backgrounds, they could not have thought of on their own.

What does trust mean in a relationship? There are several components. First, trust means that your partner will not abuse your feelings, and that you will show your feelings. Right there you are stymied, as you are entering into an arena outside your range of experience. Trusting others is one of the primary things you have guarded against since childhood, and now I am telling you that it's not going to work anymore.

One of the things that makes a good, healthy relationship so scary is that trusting is the opposite of what you have learned to do. You must trust that the person you care about will not want to hurt you, and you must show some of yourself. This is the beginning of getting to know someone in a very real way. Trust also means that you will not abuse your partner's feelings and that he/she will be able to show them to you. It goes both ways.

Secondly, trust means honesty: The other person will say what he means and mean what he says, and you will do likewise. Honesty allows you to trust the other person not to deliberately lie to you. When you reciprocate, this helps give substance to your relationship. You will know when you reach out that your hand will touch a solid arm, belonging to someone you can depend on. Your relationship won't be "fly by night," and you won't be confused.

Third, trust means that your partner will not willfully hurt you, and that you will not willfully hurt him/her. If it does happen, you will want to discuss ways to make sure it doesn't happen again. We cannot always know, when getting to know another person, what will be hurtful. It is extremely important to be able to say, "It hurt me when you said that," and for the other person to say, "It's important for me to know that; I don't want to hurt you. I will try hard not to let it happen again."

For many, trust means the promise of no physical abuse. I get angry every time I hear that an adult had such terrible childhood experiences that when we talk about trust, it automatically means they want to be rid of this fear. Physical abuse is inexcusable in any relationship. Therefore, it is non-negotiable.

Fourth, trust means the freedom to be yourself without being judged. It means that you do not have to walk on eggshells, that you can be who you are, and that the other person can be who he/she is. You are both okay. Not judging yourself and not being judged is a whole new experience, glorious and exhilarating. It is also scary as hell.

Fifth, trust means stability. There is certainty about the other person and about the relationship. It means that tomorrow's behavior will be similar to yesterday's, that you can count on things, and you can plan. It means you know that if you have plans to go somewhere on Saturday, when Saturday comes you will be able to do it. Stability, being very inconsistent with your childhood experiences, may be difficult to learn and to accept in another person.

Sixth, trust means commitment to the relationship, to the degree that the couple has agreed to be committed to the relationship. If your partner has said, "I will see only you; you are the only one with whom I am going to bed," you need to be able to believe it.

Likewise, if you have offered the same thing, you need to behave accordingly. What is important in a relationship to make you feel comfortable, once agreed upon, you can feel secure that it will be kept.

Lastly, trust means that confidences will be kept. You won't have to worry about anyone else knowing your secrets. Neither will you share the secrets of your partner. It is especially important, when you have an argument, to know that these confidences will not be used against you.

Because trust is different for different people, it can mean whatever a couple decides it means to them, individually and together.

The facets of trust I have discussed here, although essential to a healthy relationship, are difficult to build. Trusting another person doesn't happen overnight, and you needn't criticize yourself because you find it difficult. Perhaps one of the easiest ways a couple can begin to trust each other is to discuss the difficulties they have with trust and acknowledge that it is something to aim for. They need to commit themselves to working on trust on a step-by-step basis as the relationship develops. It is very important for you to recognize that trust is not something you can automatically give to another person in the depth that has been discussed here. It is important for you to know that developing trust is an essential part of the process of building a healthy relationship. At this stage, you may only hear the words and not have any idea of how to put them into practice. This is not unusual, but eventually you will learn to trust.

COA MYTH

"We will do everything together—we will be as one."

TRUTH: In the real world, couples spend time together, alone and with friends.

Boundaries

Children of Alcoholics have difficulty respecting the boundaries of others, and recognizing what their own boundaries are. You grew up in an environment where boundaries were very confusing. It was difficult to identify the respective roles of mother and father. It was hard to know if you were the child, or the mother or the father.

This confusion raises many questions. Whose pain did you feel? Was it yours? Was it your mother's? Was it your father's? Where did you end and somebody else begin?

What about privacy? What things belonged to you and could not be violated? Was your privacy invaded, even in the bathroom?

What were the limitations of good taste? What is appropriate behavior? What is inappropriate behavior?

Now that you are an adult, how do you decide if you are doing something reasonable or violating someone else's rights?

Perplexing statements and questions often come up in discussions with COAs.

"He hugged me. I felt violated. Am I wrong to feel that way?"

"I let myself in because her door was unlocked. Why did she get so bent out of shape?"

"I enjoyed the evening and invited him in for coffee. What right did he have to move in on me on the first date?"

"I worry that I will offend you. I always say the wrong thing."

"I clutch when I'm asked something personal. Isn't that *my* business?"

There is much confusion about what is intimacy and what is an invasion of boundaries. A lot of checking out is in order before you act. For example, don't do me a favor by cleaning my room unless you know I would consider it a favor. Don't insist on paying the bill after I've offered to split it, unless you know I am not invested in paying my own way. So many serious misunderstandings arise from not knowing where the other person's boundaries are. They are different for different people, and COAs, who tend to have rigid boundaries, don't understand this.

In a healthy relationship, partners try to let each other know what their boundaries are. They discuss them before the fact whenever possible, but if not then, later. For example, "I knew you meant well when you cleaned my room, but I felt enraged. That is my space, and although I would prefer it neat, it has to be my problem if it isn't."

A simple act for one person can be a major issue for another. Respecting and understanding boundaries is part of the process of becoming closer.

Boundaries and barriers are different. There is a private space that belongs to me and me alone. It is not that I choose to shut you out. It is rather that my space needs to be respected, if I am to be fully myself and fully functional.

For many, violation of that space causes irritability and a variety of physical symptoms. I develop symptoms of suffocation if my private space is violated. Others have different reactions. Some have a greater need for space and privacy than others. The issue needs to be talked about, in order to be respected and not misunderstood.

COA MYTH

"You will instinctively anticipate my every need, desire and wish."

TRUTH: In the real world, if needs, desires and wishes are not clearly communicated, it is unlikely they will be fulfilled.

Expectations

You have learned in the process of growing up with alcoholism that it is not in your best interest to have expectations. If you have an expectation, you will, at the least, be disappointed or, at most, devastated. It depends on what the promise is and how much it means to you. Unfulfilled promises run all the way from, "I'll buy you an ice cream cone," to "I'll send you to college."

You learned that the only way to protect yourself is not to expect anything from anybody. It's a rough way to live, but it's safe. You cut your losses.

But—that ever-present "but"—you also cut your gains.

Healthy relationships involve expectations. Not only do they involve expectations, they involve a shared commitment to fulfill them. The shared part is very important, because it means that you have to tell your partner what you want, and there is an agreement to attempt to meet your needs. To want flowers for your birthday and then become devastated if you don't get them is not fair to your partner, if he had no idea you expected flowers. If he knew and didn't fulfill your expectations, it is important to talk about it, because it may be a signal of difficulty in the relationship.

Many people want their partners to please them by being mind readers. That is a setup, and comes out of your fears and your questions about whether you are worth anything. If he anticipates your desires when you don't ask, you don't have to suffer over the issue of your value. If he doesn't and you don't ask, you can then put yourself down and lock in your negative feelings about yourself.

If you decide that you will express your desires and they are fulfilled, that is wonderful. But you will probably find the situation stressful, because it is unfamiliar. The body does not differentiate between dis-stress (bad) and eu-stress (good), and you, as a result, may be inclined to sabotage the relationship if it is going too smoothly. That is a response to reduce the stress, but there is the risk that you will once again begin to judge yourself negatively. After all, if you were a good person, you wouldn't do that. Good things take getting used to. Give yourself a break by allowing some time for the adjustment.

If you make your wishes clear and they are not met, it is important to understand what is going on. If the desire seems reasonable to you and it was not met, you need to find out why. You need to check it out. You may not have been clear. Your partner may not be listening to you. Your partner may be caring about you in terms of himself and not in terms of you. You may have made a demand that he could not fulfill. You might say: "If you care about me and do not express it in ways that are meaningful to me, your caring is not useful to me. It does not enhance me; it only enhances you." Once this is understood, if there is no attempt to accommodate your needs, it is a sign that the relationship is not developing in a healthy way. Either your demands are too great for your partner to meet, or your partner is too self-centered to accommodate you. This is important for you to know regardless of how the relationship is progressing. If you require a lot of nurture, you will not be satisfied in a relationship with someone who is aloof. It simply won't work.

Mutually agreed-upon expectations are essential to a

healthy relationship. Explaining away continual disappointment will not get you what you want. People do disappoint those they care about, even in healthy relationships. But it does not happen often.

Many COAs do not know what a reasonable expectation is. Is it reasonable for me to ask him to come to my door, rather than sit in the car and wait for me to come out? Is it reasonable for me to want him to wear a tie if we go out to dinner? Is it reasonable for me to ask her to share some of the expenses? A typical reaction is: Since I don't know what a reasonable expectation is, and since I don't want to look like a jerk, perhaps I should just keep my mouth shut and see what happens.

That attitude may have some validity, but it is also a way to avoid confronting an even bigger fear. Confronting the discomfort is a big step toward developing healthy intimacy. Couples develop their own norms and fulfill mutual expectations. But first, they need to be expressed and discussed.

COA MYTH

"If I am not in complete control at all times, there will be anarchy."

TRUTH: In the real world, one is in charge of one's life and takes control of situations as needed, by conscious decision and agreement. There are also times to share control and times to give up control.

Control

"If I am not in control, everything will fall apart." You learned that lesson very early. You controlled your life as best you could, because without some order there would be anarchy.

What are the implications of this approach to control in a relationship? Healthy relationships are not power struggles. They involve give and take, and shared responsibility. They also involve not having to do everything all by yourself.

To you these are just words. "I moved without asking for help from anyone!" Ann says emphatically. "Many of my friends offered to help, but I was determined to do it myself. I don't want to owe anybody anything. And nobody would care for my things the way I do."

She feels that if she accepts help, she loses control of her life. Her possessions will be ruined, and she will be forever obligated.

There is also the fear of being dependent. "If I let him help me this time, and he doesn't disappoint me, when something else comes up, I may ask him again, and pretty soon I'll become dependent on him to take care of me. Then I will no longer be able to take care of myself and I'll be stuck." This attitude implies that not being in charge at all times will lead to devastation when the inevitable abandonment occurs.

She also does not know how to share: "I know how to do it all," or, "I don't know how to do anything. Balancing responsibility is unfamiliar to me. I don't know how to do it. It may look as if I want to run everything, or as if I run away from doing my part, but it may have to do with not understanding how to work out a balance."

This is something else that needs to be talked about in very specific terms. When your partner says, "It upsets me that every time you say I can do something for you, I know you have a back-up in case I let you down," an answer might be, "It has nothing to do with you. I need a little time to accept the idea that I am not in this alone, and can give up a little control without being devastated."

An exchange such as this is double-edged, because the

need for approval and fear of abandonment are so strong in COAs that they give up emotional control. They fight for situational control, but give up their emotional selves. While declaring, "I don't need you," they don't sleep if they don't hear from you.

This kind of conflict is exhausting and requires a lot of discussion and time to process within the relationship. With work, however, it can be eased.

COA MYTH

"If we really love each other, we will stay together forever."

TRUTH: In the real world, people stay together and people separate for many reasons. You can love someone and still terminate a relationship.

Loyalty

COAs are very loyal people and offer it in all relationships. Loyalty, while an integral part of a healthy relationship, has some limitations. Loyalty is best based on a mutual decision about the limits of the relationship. Both parties decide together whether or not they want a monogamous relationship. They discuss the areas in which they feel insecure, so that the other person will not carelessly push the wrong button.

For example, if you panic when someone is five minutes late, and your partner has no sense of time, an accommodation must be worked out. If both parties respect the needs and wishes of the other, accommodations can be found. "I'll call if I'm running late," or, "Give me fifteen minutes leeway."

COAs tend to carry loyalty to an extreme. They remain in relationships they know to be destructive to them. If problems cannot be worked out, it is not a good idea to stay in the continuing fantasy that they can be resolved. That is replaying the childhood wish that life will be wonderful if only. . . . It didn't work then. It won't work now.

Loyalty in COAs is also a modeled behavior. Families enmeshed in alcoholism rarely break up until some semblance of sobriety is achieved. They stay together through thin and thinner. As a result, it is easier for you to stay with someone, even after the relationship is no longer working, than to walk away. "How can you be so callous as to hurt another person?" you ask yourself. But you dismiss the ways in which you are being hurt. You invalidate yourself.

Another aspect of this extreme loyalty comprises a

strong desire not to experience the pain of loss. Very often, a COA will have resolved all of the issues involved in ending a relationship that has become toxic. All the air has been taken out of the fantasy balloons on both the intellectual and emotional levels, and yet they do not act. "I'm still stuck! I can't move. What is wrong with me? I'm not afraid of being alone. I know I can manage. Why can't I get unstuck?"

You will have to go through a mourning period after a relationship ends. Entering into a new relationship immediately only puts it off and interferes with the new relationship. There is no way to avoid experiencing the loss. There is no way to avoid the pain. It is a part of the growth process.

In a relationship, you need to understand and be willing to work on appropriate limits to loyalty. Decide in advance what the limits are and commit yourself to remain aware of them. Recognize when you exceed them, and when something else is operating that is not in your best interest. When you start rationalizing, be aware of what you are doing; remember, it goes back to your early tapes. But, with work, you can change.

COA MYTH

"My partner will never take me for granted, and always be supportive and noncritical."

TRUTH: In the real world, things do not always go smoothly, but you always have a right to your feelings.

Validation

One of the things a COA needs most is to have his feelings validated. In your alcoholic family, your feelings were never validated. On the contrary, they were discounted with "You don't really feel that way. It's not okay to feel that way." So you start feeling peculiar about whether it is okay to feel this way or that way. You need someone who will validate your feelings—not necessarily your behavior, but your feelings.

You need someone to whom you can say, "Gee, that really made me angry. I really wanted to act like that. I really wanted to do this." And you need someone to reply, "I can appreciate those feelings. They are valid." Nobody comes into counseling, nobody goes for help, who has been validated. So it's extremely important, whatever feelings are expressed, for a partner of a COA to validate them. "Sure, you feel that way. Absolutely.

That's the way that you feel. You might want to look at it, you might want to feel differently about it. I see it differently, but it's okay to feel however you feel, and it's good for our relationship to let me know what that feeling is. The sharing makes us closer."

The sharing of feelings helps make you closer if you have established a safe climate where sharing feelings is okay. In some circumstances, the validation of feelings is critical to the development of a healthy relationship. That is, lack of validation by a partner can get in the way.

A rather extreme example of this occurred recently. A client of mine, the daughter of an alcoholic mother, is in her second marriage, to a man who has been in recovery from alcoholism for about eight months. She is not an alcoholic herself, but she is addicted to sugar. This was a difficult time in her life because her mother was dying of cancer, a long and difficult process. In addition to brain tumors and generalized cancer, her mother was suffering from advanced alcoholism. Joanie wanted to help her mother.

Although her mother had never consistently served her needs, in order for Joanie to feel good about herself, she needed to be there for her mother. If this meant visiting her mother in the hospital every night, or visiting her regularly when she was at home, it was important to Joanie that she do it. For her own sense of herself, she could not walk away from what she considered her responsibility at that time.

Joanie's husband reacted negatively to this situation. Before her mother became ill, she was a constant thorn in their sides. She did everything she could to destroy their relationship, and even her daughter. Not only that, now she was taking away the precious little time the couple had together. He was very hostile about it. "I don't like you going to visit your mother every night," he said. "We never see each other. What kind of relationship do we have?" He was very angry and jealous. You might even say he was behaving like a selfish little boy.

Her response to his behavior was very defensive. "Your attitude really stinks," she said. "My mother will be dead before long, and I need to do this for her. You and I have the rest of our lives to spend together. It is unfair of you to begrudge me this time. Your lack of understanding of my needs is absolutely appalling."

The yelling went back and forth. They were in constant conflict. She felt justified in her position, and he felt justified in his. Neither one was validating the other.

The reality here is that they do not really disagree, and that the situation was terrible. The mother's illness did take away the precious little time they had together, and it was unfortunate and uncomfortable for all of them. Joanie was spending a great deal of time with her mother, and still not getting validated. The fact that her mother was dying did not serve any of Joanie's needs. So, once again, Joanie was giving and giving.

It would be ideal if her husband were in a stage of his own development where he could be supportive to her, but he was not. It would also be ideal if Joanie were in a stage of her own recovery where she did not have to devote herself totally to her mother, but she was not. If this couple were able to validate each other, the friction that existed between them would virtually disappear.

Joanie needed to say to her husband, "I agree with you. You are absolutely right. My mother *is* a pain in the ass. You and I are not spending enough time together, and she is taking away from the precious little time that we have together. Yes, I am resentful that I need to do this for myself, and that I haven't reached a point where I can be more reasonable in serving my mother's needs." If she were able to validate his feelings instead of defending her mother and defending her right to be there for her mother, they would not be in conflict. She would not have to behave any differently. She would be capable of saying, "I wish I were able to be less compulsive about this, and that I could serve both our needs and my mother's needs. I wish I were further along in my growth."

Once she had validated his feelings, he would no longer have to feel as defensive and then neither would she. He could then validate her feelings with something like, "I am glad you understand how I feel. It really makes me angry, but I can also understand how there will be no living with you if you do not do what you see as your responsibility right now."

Validation can be the key to getting through a crisis. Without validation, it is quite possible that the damage done to the relationship will be irreparable. She won't be able to forgive him for his "stinking thinking," and he won't be able to forgive her for abandoning him when he wanted and needed her.

This story does have a happy ending. They did validate each other, and the pressure on their relationship eased. One afternoon, when Joanie was visiting her mother but unobserved by her, she overheard her mother tell the nurse things she had never told Joanie. She told the nurse how much she loved Joanie, how proud she was of her, and how appreciative she was of her care and attention.

When Joanie told her mother she had overheard the conversation, they cried together, shared the depth of

READER/CUSTOMER CARE SURVEY

We care about your opinions! Please take a moment to fill out our online Reader Survey at **http://survey.hcibooks.com**.

As a **"THANK YOU"** you will receive a **VALUABLE INSTANT COUPON** towards future book purchases as well as a **SPECIAL GIFT** available only online! Or, you may mail this card back to us and we will send you a copy of our exciting catalog with your valuable coupon inside.

(PLEASE PRINT IN ALL CAPS)

First Name _____ MI. _____ Last Name _____

Address _____ City _____

State _____ Zip _____ Email _____

1. Gender
- ❏ Female ❏ Male

2. Age
- ❏ 8 or younger
- ❏ 9-12 ❏ 13-16
- ❏ 17-20 ❏ 21-30
- ❏ 31+

3. Did you receive this book as a gift?
- ❏ Yes ❏ No

4. Annual Household Income
- ❏ under $25,000
- ❏ $25,000 - $34,999
- ❏ $35,000 - $49,999
- ❏ $50,000 - $74,999
- ❏ over $75,000

5. What are the ages of the children living in your house?
- ❏ 0 - 14 ❏ 15+

6. Marital Status
- ❏ Single
- ❏ Married
- ❏ Divorced
- ❏ Widowed

7. How did you find out about the book?
(please choose one)
- ❏ Recommendation
- ❏ Store Display
- ❏ Online
- ❏ Catalog/Mailing
- ❏ Interview/Review

8. Where do you usually buy books?
(please choose one)
- ❏ Bookstore
- ❏ Online
- ❏ Book Club/Mail Order
- ❏ Price Club (Sam's Club, Costco's, etc.)
- ❏ Retail Store (Target, Wal-Mart, etc.)

9. What subject do you enjoy reading about the most?
(please choose one)
- ❏ Parenting/Family
- ❏ Relationships
- ❏ Recovery/Addictions
- ❏ Health/Nutrition
- ❏ Christianity
- ❏ Spirituality/Inspiration
- ❏ Business Self-help
- ❏ Women's Issues
- ❏ Sports

10. What attracts you most to a book?
(please choose one)
- ❏ Title
- ❏ Cover Design
- ❏ Author
- ❏ Content

FOLD HERE

Comments

their love, and her mother was then able to die well because she had finally begun to live well.

Validation does not mean agreement. It means respect for similarities and differences. It is the cornerstone of good, solid communication. Without validation, communication is merely a power play.

Issues of Sexuality

Same-Sex Relationships

COAs' concerns about having healthy, intimate relationships are the same in same-sex relationships as those in opposite-sex relationships. These concerns, however, are compounded because of the difficulties involved in being homosexual in a culture that is largely homophobic. Though the issues are the same for those involved in same-sex relationships, they are exaggerated by the larger culture. The ability to share oneself openly, honestly and freely, without fear of the consequences, is impaired by living in an alcoholic home. Learned defensive behaviors have to be turned around in order to have a healthy relationship, especially for the homosexual, whose need for defenses has been reinforced in the mainstream.

Clients I see who are involved in same-sex relationships fall roughly into three categories. First, there are
those who have been aware of their sexual preference for
as long as they can remember, and have spent time and
energy dealing with, and coming to grips with, what that
reality means to them. For these people, the struggle is
the same as for those involved in opposite-sex relationships, except that the struggle may be more pronounced.

The second group consists of those who are just
becoming aware of their sexuality. They are people of all
ages, who have just admitted on a conscious level that
they have a same-sex preference. Many of the symptoms
they have carried with them during their lives begin to
disappear. One symptom is depression, which, for many,
once they have acknowledged their sexual preference,
begins to abate. This group is very similar to the blos-
soming adolescent who is becoming aware of himself as a
sexual being for the first time and is excited about it,
afraid of it, and has to test it out by going through many
experiences to find out how things work. This person
experiences the great joy and great pain of the adolescent
extremes. The age may seem inappropriate, but one must
go through all of these stages, regardless of when the
awareness hits. An additional complication may arise
from the fact that many of these people are married, have

children, and have complicated lives in the heterosexual world. They need to make decisions as to how best to handle the rest of their lives.

The third group consists of those who have decided that, because they have had such horrendous relationships with the opposite sex, starting invariably with the parent of the opposite sex, that they do not want to repeat the experience. As a result, they decide they will become involved only in same-sex relationships. Needless to say, this does not work. Whether or not an individual has or does not have a penis does not mean that he will not have the same personality type as that of those you have been involved with before, or as your mother or father. It has been my experience that people who run to same-sex relationships as a way of avoiding repetition of the horrors of their past run the risk of picking the same personality type they picked in heterosexual relationships.

The important consideration here is that they come to grips with the underlying issues from which they are fleeing. A healthy choice of a partner is possible, regardless of sex.

The essentials for intimacy for lesbians and gay men who are COAs are no different from those in opposite-sex relationships. The difficulties are compounded by society, but the struggle is the same.

General Sexual Issues

What happens to a couple in the sexual part of their relationship is symptomatic of everything else that is happening. The issues present here show up in other places, as sexual intimacy is one means of communicating and sharing oneself.

The questions I hear are endless: What's normal? How long does it take to be in synch sexually? Is it a good idea to be honest about sexual experiences and attitudes? Am I any good? Am I good enough? Can sex be fun? Is there a lot to know? How do I keep from holding back? If I'm free, will I be more vulnerable? Am I seen only as a sex object? Do I have to give up control?

Ask the questions. Read the literature. Talk about sex with your partner. Find out what works for you. The couple decides what is normal, and it is a shared learning experience. Discuss the things that get in the way. Some are easily resolved, while others that are historically based will take time to overcome. The parental relationship you saw in your childhood was distorted in many ways, including the sex life. It may have influenced you in ways that make your sexual adjustment difficult, and leave you with questions about your sexuality. You may be as confused about your sexuality as you are about other aspects of your life.

Celebration of yourself in any aspect of your life is difficult. So you need to take a look at what sex means to you. One client said, "My parents fought. Then they had sex, and everything was fine. I always understood sex was a way to end an argument, but I knew there had to be something wrong with that." The missing piece is that there was no resolution of the conflict. Sex was used as a way to avoid problem-solving, rather than to enhance the relationship.

Here is another example: "My mother told me having sex was a woman's duty. It wasn't pleasurable, but it put men to sleep. I don't want that for myself, but I feel guilty if I don't perform when asked."

To resolve these feelings, a couple should talk about their sexual relationship, especially their expectations.

Again, "Sex was always a control and power issue in my house. It was linked to physical abuse. I am so afraid it will happen to me, that I remain celibate."

This is a deep and serious problem that needs to be worked out with a therapist. A caring partner can help, but more is probably necessary in a case like this.

Many men and women have reported an inability to climax. When explored, it becomes clear that there is a holding back in other areas of the relationship as well. It is a fear of being vulnerable, because being vulnerable has always meant pain. It is a very clear demonstration of how the lack of risk-taking can limit an experience.

Alcoholism results in even more complex problems. Martha related the following: "My father cheated on my mother, and my two alcoholic husbands cheated on me. As a result, I don't want to get sexually involved with anyone, because I don't think I could go through that again. I think that's probably one of the reasons why I have gained all of this weight."

A discussion of alcoholics, and the need for alcoholics to have enablers, will not work with this lady. She has decided on a deep level that it is her own lack of desirability that caused her husbands to be unfaithful. Somehow she also finds herself responsible for her father's philandering. Putting on a lot of weight is a way to avoid the issue: If no one finds her sexually desirable, then she does not have to deal with the issue. Fortunately, she is working with a good therapist who will help her discover her sexual self, and recognize that the difficulty lies not in her lack of desirability, but in her selection of a partner. As she changes and grows, her choices will be more compatible with what she really wants.

In healthy relationships, decisions about monogamy evolve as the relationship progresses. When people are first getting to know each other, it is not unusual for them to be involved with others, too. As the relationship develops, they make decisions about exclusivity. When alcoholism is involved, the rules get shifted. Early on, there is monogamy, but as the disease progresses, it is not unusual for the alcoholic to seek out other partners.

Another problem I hear is, "The only place that I feel powerful and in control is in the bedroom. I begin to believe that that is the only thing that I have to offer another person. It makes me very sad." Take heart. If you are capable of being a good partner in the bedroom, you are capable of being a good partner in other aspects of the relationship. What goes on in the bedroom generalizes to other places.

Being technically good is something else again. If you are merely technically good, we are not talking about a relationship. In a relationship, emotional investment and caring are primary. You have probably not given yourself enough credit for being able to express your feelings. The bedroom may be a place where you can do that. Somehow, you have used your freedom in this area as another means of beating yourself rather than using it to celebrate yourself. The opposite is also true. "I love my husband very much. He is very dear to me, and we are good friends as well as being man and wife. I want to share my entire life with him, but I don't want to make love to him. In my house, lovemaking was like violation. I am terrified that this is what it will evolve into."

When I talked to Lynn about lovemaking, it became clear that she was talking about intercourse. When I asked her if she enjoyed having her husband say affectionate things to her, or having him put his arms around her, she said, "Oh, yes." When I asked her if they just ever held hands when they went for a walk, she said she enjoyed that, too. The reality here is that they make love in a variety of ways. Because of her childhood experience, she mistakenly equated intercourse with lovemaking, and was not able to see the larger picture. As she became aware of the many aspects of lovemaking that she shared with her husband, she was free from the notion that she would repeat her parents' negative relationship.

The variations on these themes are endless. The underlying problem is, "I am afraid of being close." As you work out other aspects of allowing yourself to be close, the sexual part will work out, too. If you find that this area still presents difficulties, it may be time to work with a professional who can help you overcome them. Sex is only one aspect of a relationship. Yet, the shared closeness can be very important and very significant.

Overcoming the distortions resulting from your child-hood is important to your personal growth. Remember, here, too, you do not have enough information to answer all of your questions. This a probably a large part of what is getting in your way.

Take it easy on yourself. Take it easy on your partner. Once again, the message is—go slowly. In fact, no aspect of a healthy relationship happens overnight. The poten-tial may be immediately obvious, but a relationship is a day-to-day developing experience.

Incest

Although incest is not necessarily part of a family sys-tem affected by alcohol, it is present frequently enough to warrant discussion.

Incest is a much more widespread manifestation of dysfunction in families than we have yet begun to explore. The family system where alcoholism is present is a fertile ground for it to occur. There is no doubt that COAs who are survivors of incest have an additional dimension of great difficulty in establishing healthy, intimate relationships.

Although incest occurs between mothers and sons, fathers and sons, and among siblings, the most common form is between fathers and daughters. The latter will therefore be the focus of discussion here.

Incest can be overt or covert. Overt incest is defined simply as sexual contact within the family. Though not necessarily actual intercourse, it involves sexual contact in one form or another. The most usual forms involve fondling of breasts and genitals, use of the child to mas-turbate and oral sex. Covert incest involves many of the same dynamics, but there is no actual physical contact.

Many of the conditions present in other incestuous families are also present in the alcoholic family system. Certainly the taboo against talking about what is going on exists, as does isolation of the family. In many inces-tuous families, as in many families where alcoholism is present, one of the daughters, usually the oldest, has taken over many of the responsibilities of running the household and looking after the younger children. Fulfilling her father sexually may be looked upon as an extension of the role of "little mother." There is a greater likelihood that this behavior will occur if there is a role reversal between mother and daughter. This role reversal happens often when the mother is chronically ill or alcoholic.

How does incest relate to later intimate relationships? First, the ability to trust, which has been discussed earlier, is destroyed. The most outrageous aspect of an incestuous relationship precludes a "safe harbor." The child has no one to run to.

I have asked many clients who were incest survivors why they didn't tell someone. "Why did you wait until your late twenties or early thirties to let someone know that you were abused as a child?" Invariably, the response is, "What good would it have done? If I had told my mother, it would have made no difference. She would not have believed me, or dealt with it. It would only have made circumstances worse. I certainly could not have gone to anyone outside the family." These children had no place to turn, no one to help them.

So here is a circumstance where you found out at a very early age that there was no one to trust. You certainly could not trust the parent who was sexually abusing you, nor the other parent. So you learned that the only one you could trust was yourself. Because of this early and generally continuing experience, what you learned is quite clear. First, you learned from living with alcoholism that you cannot trust, because if you do, you will be hurt. Moreover, you learned that there is no one to trust. This early experience greatly exaggerates the difficulty you have later on in trusting someone in an intimate relationship.

Second, incest affects your present sexual behavior. It is not unusual for incest survivors in a sexual relationship with another person to flashback on the horrors of their childhood. They will flashback while in a loving relationship to the experiences of childhood, and this causes problems.

Third, some survivors of incest believe they can only obtain love and affection through sex. If the sexual experience with the father was pleasurable, they see themselves as having tremendous sexual powers. This fantasy distorts the development of a healthy, intimate relationship. It also leads to idealizing men.

Fourth, many decide to involve themselves in same-sex relationships, because they never again want to face the dreaded penis. However, the other distortions and difficulties continue to come into play. The difficulty of trusting does not go away because you are involved in a same-sex relationship. Neither parent could be trusted. So this, in and of itself, is not a solution to the problem.

When incest is covert, rather than overt, some of the same circumstances apply. The father treats the little girl like his wife or his love object. He is jealous of her suitors and makes subtle sexual innuendoes. She does many of the things that, in other circumstances, his wife might do. The result here is somewhat different. The child doesn't feel abused: She feels idealized. She also idealizes the parent, which makes it extremely difficult for her to relate to other men. Because her daddy is the perfect love object, she seeks out men who are like her father in an attempt to replace him.

This is a very difficult bond to break. How can you want to pull away from someone who makes you feel so special? How can you find someone else who will adore you unconditionally? The pain of working this through is excruciating. Although your sexual fantasies have not been experienced in the real world, they may be powerful enough to keep you from appreciating someone else. It is a mistake to underestimate the hold of a covertly incestuous relationship.

The child's reaction to the violation of incest is on a very deep level and must be addressed on that level. With many of the issues concerned with living in an alcoholic home, the mere flushing them out by discussion with people who understand, who have had the same experiences, goes a long way toward resolving them.

However, this is not usually the case with incest, so it is very important to work this out with a professional. You must come to grips with the guilt and shame that incest survivors feel. Somehow there is always the sense that "I am responsible." "Why does it happen to me and not to my sister?" Or, "If it happened to both my sister and me, why didn't I do anything to prevent it?" Since children are compliant in an alcoholic family system, when they reflect back, they see themselves as going along with it, as being willing, as not fighting against incest. They feel responsibility, which is neither valid nor true.

Today, you would not permit this kind of behavior, but the adult you are now did not exist when you were a child. Take a look at yourself as a small child, and tell her she is guilty for what happened. It is not possible. Relieving the guilt, however, is not as easy as intellectually understanding that you could not have been responsible. For many who have taken over the role of the mother, it is even a protection of her. This is similar to a child taking a beating for other siblings or the mother, so the others will not have to endure it. At any rate, you were not responsible. The guilt you feel because you were powerless to stop incest from happening is inappropriate. You had no choice, because you knew no alternatives.

The shame you feel is also inappropriate. The sense of yourself as a disgusting person, as someone who experienced incest because you were disgusting, is not true. You were not disgusting. You were a victim, and you were trapped. You need to work out these feelings of shame in order to feel good about yourself. Otherwise, your shame will get in the way of developing a healthy sexual relationship, where you can celebrate your body as wholesome and good.

Do not try to do this alone. Today there are many therapists who specialize in working with incest survivors. It is important to work with someone who is not only sensitive to the alcoholic family system, but sensitive to what happens to children who have been sexually abused. I cannot emphasize this strongly enough, because the pathology of sexual abuse is deeper than the results of alcoholism. I am not, however, minimizing the pain and struggle that one has for the rest of one's life, as a result of living in an alcoholic home.

You are not alone. You will be flabbergasted, once you begin to share your experience, at how many others have also been through it. Just as keeping the secret of living with alcoholism was not to your advantage, keeping the secret of incest works against you. Sharing this secret can be the start of setting you free. It is in no way a reflection on you that you had a parent who was sick enough to use you in this way.

So You Love a COA

It is not surprising to me that you have fallen in love with a COA. Children of Alcoholics are the most loving and loyal people around. They offer more than any other group of people I know. I am certain that you, too, are impressed at what they are able to offer in a relationship, or you would not be involved with a COA.

A relationship with a COA is also very confusing to you, I am sure. Just when you think everything is fine, just when you think that the relationship is the most fantastic, beautiful, intense, intimate, exciting experience of your life, your COA will back off. You will not know what hit you. When you think you have a thorough understanding, he or she will do something contrary. Many times your COA will react in ways that seem peculiar to you, in ways that make absolutely no sense. Naturally, you will find yourself confused. This section is designed to help you better understand what goes on in your partner's mind. More often than not, your partner's peculiar behavior has nothing to do with you, although your behavior may trigger it.

I am not telling you to behave differently unless it is useful for both you and your partner for mutual behaviors to be modified. This discussion is to let you know what is going on, so that your reactions in a given situation will be more responsive to what is really happening to your COA.

Understanding what makes your partner tick will be very useful. When COAs respond peculiarly to situations, it is often because they do not know how to react differently. They do not know that there are other options, and they do not know what is appropriate. Many times I hear, "How could I do the right thing, if I don't know what right is?" It may be that there are no "rights." But there are certainly responses which are appropriate.

For example, people who have typical backgrounds can more easily confront others than those who come from alcoholic homes. If you are in a restaurant and the person at the next table is smoking, which is offensive to you, it is natural to ask him to put out the cigarette or blow the smoke in another direction. Your COA, on the other hand, may start squirming in the chair or become terrified. Your COA has many feelings that would never occur to you. Depending on the history, there might be a great deal of fear, along with a sense of protection toward you, and an overwhelming sense of gratitude to you for taking care of the situation.

Confrontation is never easy for Children of Alcoholics. And it is especially difficult for them to con-front you in an intimate relationship. It is also not easy for them to observe you confronting someone else, regardless of how insignificant the confrontation is. I am not saying don't do it. Simply be aware of the possibility that the reaction may be something different from what you anticipate.

Several bottomline fears Children of Alcoholics have will affect their responses to you. Your understanding can help alleviate them. I am not suggesting that all COAs have all of these fears, but they probably have one or more of them.

Fear Number 1: "I am afraid that I will hurt you."

This fear results from the fact that COAs are not taught how to speak and behave appropriately. The behaviors they develop result from watching others.

Although many of them do behave appropriately, and many are very clever, charming and articulate, they don't really believe they are. They are afraid they will violate your boundaries. They are afraid that, without meaning to, they will say something or behave in a way that will be hurtful to you. If they do these things, it is not deliberate, but because they don't know there are alternatives. As a result, COAs tend not to be spontaneous, and you may frequently sense that they are holding back. This is something worth checking out. You might say to the COA you are involved with, "Let's take the risk. If you do or say something that hurts me, I will tell you, just as I want you to tell me if I do something that hurts you. This is the only way we can really get to know each other and be attentive to each other's feelings."

Fear Number 2: "The person you see does not exist."

Children of Alcoholics are so concerned with trying to look and behave normally that, in many ways, they fabricate the person they would like to be, or the kind of person they think you would like them to be. Chances are, this mask does not work as well as they think it does. You are probably able to see who he or she really is, and that is who you are attracted to. This is difficult for the COA to believe. The outside looks good. While outside behavior is exciting and interesting, however, inside there is fear and trembling. Although both parts of the person are valid and true, the COA feels that the outer side that looks confident is not real, and the inner self that is frightened is the real self. Therefore, you have been fooled into believing the inner self does not exist. Ideally, it would be good for the COA to express his or her fears, and have self-confidence. Though both parts of the person exist, the COA is not sure you see him or her as he/she really is. Worse yet, if you did, you would no longer find him/her interesting and attractive. The desirable, interesting, attractive, intelligent, charming, sexual person with whom you believe you are involved does not really exist in his/her mind.

Fear Number 3: "I'll lose control of my life."

"My mother was out of control; my father was out of control; and they were in control of me. What a terrible thought! What a horrible memory! I cannot let it happen again. Since I am so unsure of myself, I am afraid that if I get close to you, I will defer to you in all things. I will let you make all the decisions, because I am afraid

I will make the wrong ones. I really don't want to do that, but I am uncertain I will be strong enough not to give in. Therefore, I will back away from you, or make preposterous demands that you cannot possibly fulfill in order to prove to myself that you want control."

To counteract this problem, you have to sit down as a couple and work on decision-making. COAs do not have a strong sense of what alternatives and consequences are. Discuss the options involved, and come to some mutual agreements. Your impatience at indecision, although certainly understandable, will not help your partner make a decision. You may have to allow time to work things through together, and find out if the COA has all of the information necessary to make the decision. You might need to say to your partner, "I am making this decision, because there is a time limit. However, that does not mean I am trying to control our relationship. It means only that a decision has to be made." Things that are shared up front are less frightening and can be viewed more realistically.

Fear Number 4: "It doesn't matter anyway."

This is a very defensive position. It comes from a depressed attitude learned in the alcoholic family system, which develops into a depressed lifestyle. When one is depressed, one feels that nothing really matters. This attitude is also somewhat protective: "If I decide that it doesn't matter anyway, then I will be less hurt if something goes wrong. If I allow it to matter, then I will be devastated if something goes wrong." It is also a way of testing. A COA who has this attitude will test you repeatedly to be sure that you will not leave. You may have to confront your partner, saying, "This is a game. I care about you. You do not have to continue to test me." If you don't say anything, and the testing continues, eventually you will leave: You won't be able to handle it.

The testing, however, is not selfishness or wanting to put you through your paces. It comes from insecurity and a rather poor self-image, which only time can cure. Gradually, the defenses will ease up. "It doesn't matter" is akin to "I don't exist," and "If I am not around, you will forget all about me." This is a setup for you to continue to prove that you care. Once you see it as such, you might ask, "How many times do I have to tell you?" "How much more do I need to show you?"

Fear Number 5: "It's not real."

Your COA may have said to you on many occasions, "This is not real. This is not really happening." He makes these statements when things are going well—when the relationship you share is something that you find so wonderful and so fine and so rare that you can hardly believe it. Not believing it is different from not seeing it as real. Not believing it involves real excitement and a sense of incredulousness: "How lucky I am to have found this person with whom I can share and experience so much!" That's probably what you mean when you say, "This is not really happening to me. How fortunate I am!"

When your COA says, "This is not real," it means something different. For many COAs, growing up was so traumatic that this is the only reality they know. When life is going well, the circumstances are so unfamiliar they have a sense of unreality about them. So the effect is unsettling.

When you are walking on clouds and believe that your partner is right there beside you, he or she may do something to sabotage the relationship. All of a sudden, out of the blue, your COA will pick a fight with you or not answer your phone calls. This kind of thing makes absolutely no sense to you, and you feel pushed away. If things are that wonderful, they cannot be real, so the COA, in order to make them real, will use sabotage.

Since you now know this, you can feel a little less punched in the stomach. You can recognize that an unpleasant reaction does not have to do with you, but with the COA's learned responses. You might simply say, "I have not done anything. Things are good. Just try and relax and go slowly." If your COA runs away, chances are he or she will be back. You will probably need to do something in order to protect yourself, but realize that the rejection is only temporary. Your understanding will help keep the situation from getting more complicated.

When COAs realize what they have done, they feel very guilty and remorseful, and decide that you couldn't continue to love them anyway, because they are terrible people. If they weren't so terrible, they could enjoy things going well, and wouldn't get in the way of their own happiness, etc. If you can just roll with it, chances are you can ride this one out, too.

Fear Number 6: "You'll see how angry I am."

COAs learn to repress their anger. They learn as children that if they express anger like other kids do, it will only create more difficulty. As a result, many are filled with unresolved anger. There is a real fear that the anger felt towards their parents and their backgrounds will leak out in a relationship. They are afraid that their anger will be directed at you in inappropriate ways. They are also afraid that if you see the extent of that anger, it will frighten you away. This may or may not be true, according to your own reactions to anger, and to what degree you are concerned about other people's reactions to you.

Things happen in a relationship that will trigger off early experiences. It is important for you and your COA to know each other well. Then, when something happens which you don't understand on the face of it, you will realize that it relates back to childhood. When your COA reacts with inappropriate anger to a situation, chances are that the degree of anger does not relate to what is going on in the moment.

Sarah asked Tommy if he would move some branches that had fallen off her tree from her front yard to her backyard. They were too heavy for her to carry, and it was not difficult for him. He said he would be very happy to do it for her. When she returned from work and saw that it had not been done, she went into a rage. He was flabbergasted at how angry she was, but said, "I'm sorry. I forgot all about it, but I will get it done for you." It is clear that since she was ready to end the relationship over such a minor thing, she was overreacting. But, if you look at Sarah's reaction in the context of her being a COA, the incident has a great deal of meaning.

First, it was a struggle to ask him to do her a favor. It

was very hard for her to say, "I need help with the work."
She has learned not to ask for favors, because they were
never granted. But, since she is working on this important relationship, she made a conscious decision to ask.

She is also overly concerned about what her neighbors
will think if her yard is messy. This consciousness of
other people's opinion of her indicates she is not yet
secure with her opinion of herself. When Tommy forgot,
she felt completely invalidated by him. Her reasoning
went like this: If he really cared about me, he would recognize that I would not ask him to do anything that was
not important to me, and he would not forget. Not forgetting to remove the wood means that he cares about
me. Forgetting to remove the wood means that I am not
as important to him as he pretends I am.

Certainly, the extent of her anger at him is inappropriate. There is cause for annoyance, but not for the rage
that she feels. He was insensitive to her needs in taking
her request so casually. He was responding to his own history, to the fact that he procrastinates.

This couple needs to discuss this incident thoroughly in
order for the relationship to remain healthy. She needs
to understand that every request will not automatically be
responded to, even though it is difficult for her to ask.
She also needs to understand that his procrastination

is not a reflection of his feelings for her. If his behavior continues, and it is something that she cannot live with, then she may need to reassess the relationship. But, on the face of it, her reaction seems more powerful than the circumstance called for.

Tommy will have to learn that if he agrees to do something, he must do it on the terms of the person who asked him to do it. If he tells her, "Yes, I will do it for you," and understands her urgency, then it is unfair of him not to fulfill the request as it is asked. If he is not certain that he can do what is asked immediately, it is important for him to say, "I will do it for you, but I cannot promise that I will do it right now."

Communication and discussion of feelings are critical for COAs, and the people with whom they are involved. It is the only way to have a healthy relationship.

Fear Number 7: "I am ashamed of who I am."

You may be shocked when you become aware of how low an opinion the COA with whom you are involved has of him/herself. It may be nearly impossible for you to understand how this bright, charming, capable, lovable person can see him/herself as such SHIT! Though it makes no sense to you at all, it is real and a deep, dark secret.

The reason for this level of shame is that many COAs believe they were responsible for the dysfunction in their families. Many were told from the beginning, "Life was great until you came along." "If you weren't such a brat, I wouldn't be drinking." Not only did many believe that they were responsible for the alcoholism, but as they grew older and understood that alcoholism was a disease, they became disgusted with themselves because they were still angry with their parents and humiliated by their behavior.

The message they gave themselves was, "I must be a very disgusting person if I feel this way about a person who is sick."

It may be that your COA has not invited you to see his/her family, and you wonder why. This could be part of the reason. Your COA might be humiliated, while judging him/herself for feeling this way. At the same time, he/she is very concerned about what you think— whether you will continue to care if you know what the family situation is like. Although these feelings of responsibility and shame are inappropriate, that does not mean they don't exist. This lovely adult whom you have come to know and care about is still beating him/herself for childhood experiences over which he/she had no control. Your discovery of this secret causes fear in

COAs. Once the secret is out in the open, it may lose some power. But the attitude is so deeply rooted, it perpetuates a sense of "If you really knew me, you wouldn't want to have anything to do with me."

Fear Number 8: "You will get to know me and find out that I am not lovable."

This fear is closely allied to shame. The feeling of not being lovable was learned in early childhood.

The child wanted to find a way to make things okay, to fix them. No matter what he/she did, it was not good enough. No matter how hard he/she tried, it did not matter. The child, a powerless victim of the situation, believed that there was something wrong with him/her because he/she could not find a way to fix it. If he/she were truly lovable, he/she would find a way to make life fine and happy once again. Many COAs have cried in my arms: "I tried to stop it, I tried to make it different, but I just couldn't. And the worst thing of all is that sometimes when my parents were fighting, I didn't even get in the middle of it, because I was terrified that I would be next. How could I be lovable if I was thinking about myself first?"

The truth is that the person you care about is lovable.

It will be hard for him/her to accept that. You will need to be patient. It takes time for a self-perception to change.

Fear Number 9: "I want to be comfortable."

The person you care about may back away from an involvement with you by using the argument, "I want to be comfortable." This may make absolutely no sense. The rationale goes something like this: "My whole life has been one series of emotional crises after another. I'm tired of it. I don't want it. I don't want to feel any more. Feelings are very disruptive to me. If I get involved with you, I'm bound to feel. I'm bound to feel ups and downs, and right now I have my whole life in order, and don't want to risk screwing it up. Getting involved with you would not allow me to maintain the even keel I'm on now. I will begin to care, and then I'll feel upset. I'll begin to feel a whole variety of things. I don't want that right now! I want to feel comfortable."

This attitude won't last long. It is a fantasy that many ACOAs have when they go through a level period. It won't last, not only because they are active, vibrant people, but because they have no frame of reference for it.

Being comfortable will become extremely boring, and they cannot sustain it. The reality is that the development of a healthy relationship will afford them a level of comfort that has not been experienced before. But that is a long process, requiring much hard work.

Fear Number 10: "You'll leave me anyway."

Your COA may be afraid to get involved because of fear of abandonment. The fear that the person with whom he/she is involved will walk out on him/her is absolutely terrifying. This fear is different from the fear of rejection. Fear of abandonment is much deeper: "If you abandon me and I am left all by myself, I will die."

This, too, has its roots in childhood, and not in the real world. It results in an initial fear of getting involved at all. But once the decision is made to become involved, you may find that your COA is very possessive, jealous and insecure where you are concerned. This disconcerting behavior comes from fear of abandonment. It is a big problem, because if this possessiveness gets out of hand, you may be forced to do exactly what your partner fears the most. It is therefore important for you to continue to reassure your COA that you do care, that you are not going to leave, but that it's important for you to have other people in your life. It is also important for your partner to have other people in his/her life. Rather than harming a relationship, other friends enhance it. You may need to reinforce this idea many, many times, at the same time being aware that the possessiveness comes from a very basic fear of abandonment.

You also need to be careful not to disappoint your partner. Other people react much more casually when you forget to call, or are an hour late. But COAs tend to overreact to this kind of behavior; they begin to panic. You need to understand this, so your relationship can develop, flourish and provide the security necessary to both of you.

You may be wondering at this point whether or not it's worth struggling with all the fears I have outlined. Try to bear a few things in mind. First, not all COAs suffer from all of these fears. Second, not all people are free from these fears, even though they did not grow up with alcoholism. Third, COAs' greatest difficulties are in the area of their relationship with themselves. Their greatest difficulty is the lack of ability to experience themselves as valuable and worthy and lovable. Their greatest assets are a capability of offering *you* the sense that *you* are valuable and worthy and lovable. There is much to be gained from being involved with a COA. The difficulties you face can be overcome if both members of the partnership are willing to work on them. With awareness and understanding come the potential for resolution of most difficulties.

Knowing the characteristics shared by many ACOAs can help give a direction to effect change. Being able to pinpoint areas of difficulty makes it easier to offer options to make the struggle for a healthier relationship that much easier.

Getting It All Together

1. Adult Children of Alcoholics guess at what normal is.

You have probably decided that you are *not* going to have the kind of relationship your parents had. Whatever else you do in your life, that is a no-no. However, you won't get off that easy!

Since you have decided that you will not have what you experienced at home, what will you have? Where will you get your role models? You got it! The media—*The Brady Bunch*—*Eight Is Enough*—or *Father Knows Best!* You might have picked a family down the block that does everything together and that you think is ideal. All of these are fantasies. If you have any of these notions about ideal family relationships, you have set yourself up for failure. At the very least, you will be disillusioned.

First, no woman can, for a sustained period of time, bake the bread, be an ideal mother, keep an immaculate house, maintain a career, be a sex object and helpmate, have no problems of her own, and always lend a willing ear. Neither can a man be a perfect father, pursue a career thirteen to fourteen hours a day, keep all the repairs up to date, be attentive and appreciative at all times, and pay the bills without a word of worry or complaint.

Because you decided this is the opposite of what happened at home, you try to be "perfect." The result of behaving this way is not sainthood and appreciation; it is burnout and resentment.

What is normal in a relationship is behavior that is reasonable and comfortable for you as a couple. Normalcy means discussing and working through behaviors that cause discomfort. People have different strengths and weaknesses, so there is no mold into which one must fit. A couple defines their own norms, according to what works for them.

Outside stresses will intervene and upset the balance, but you, as a couple, will address those issues as well. If you know couples who have relationships you admire, talk to them: Find out what works for them—then decide if any of it is useful to you.

2. Adult Children of Alcoholics have difficulty following a project through from beginning to end.

A relationship is very much like a project in that it involves a process. For the same reason that you have had difficulty following through on a project from beginning to end, you will have difficulty in developing a relationship. Keep in mind that healthy relationships develop slowly; they do not happen overnight. Remember the alcoholism in your family. It, too, developed slowly. Things that are good for you develop slowly as well.

It is important to recognize that in a relationship the critical part is the journey. The Alcoholics Anonymous slogans "Easy Does It" and "One Day at a Time" apply to relationships as well as to everything else. Though it is very hard to be patient, there is no other alternative. You cannot know everything about each other in a short time, no matter how intense you were in the beginning. It doesn't matter that you spent all day and all night together over a weekend. You cannot know what a long-term day-to-day relationship is like until you experience it. You need time to develop a healthy relationship.

When you were a child, you were completely vulnerable,

trusting and you gave all. That is what children do. As you got a little older, you learned how to hold back a little of yourself. That was important for your own survival. Now you say, "I will no longer give 100 percent. I will give maybe 80 percent or maybe 75 percent, but I am incapable of giving 100 percent." It is important for you to change your usual style of making a great emotional investment in the beginning. Instead, decide ahead of time on some limitations.

Other people do not have to make this kind of decision. It comes naturally to do it slowly; in the initial stages of the relationship, they invest 10 percent or 15 percent. As the relationship develops, the investment grows as well. It grows according to what both people put into it.

Do not start out at the end of the scale, where you give all that you have. Let your investment in the relationship develop naturally over time. During this process, you will reach a decision about how much is appropriate for you to give.

3. Adult Children of Alcoholics lie when it would be just as easy to tell the truth.

It is important to realize that you may lie automatically. This is not going to be useful if you want a healthy relationship. Chances are that you hold back on the truth with respect to your feelings, and not much else. Be careful that you don't set yourself up so your partner is suspicious of everything that comes out of your mouth. You might simply say, "Sometimes I am not honest in reporting the way I feel, but when I realize it, I want to be able to tell you at a later time that I didn't say what I meant." It could be helpful to write down the things you want to say. If you tend to be defensive and dishonest in situations where you want to be honest, write down what you want to say and then read it to your partner. "This is what I want to tell you. Let me just read it and we'll take it from there." You may be able to trust written communication more than the spontaneous words that come out of your mouth. As you become more comfortable and secure in the relationship, it will be easier to change your habit of not saying what you mean.

4. Adult Children of Alcoholics judge themselves without mercy.

Be aware of the fact that your inclination is to automatically find fault with yourself. Rather than finding fault with yourself or with your partner, try to look at issues and circumstances and make decisions on the basis of them. If you or your partner behave in ways that you are unhappy with, step back, take a look at the behavior, and try to understand what it means. If you can be objective, you will be able to look at the situation differently and judge it less. This will be a struggle, because your automatic inclination is to judge. Become fascinated with yourself and your responses. You are a very interesting person. The more you look at how you behave, the more skilled you will become in getting to know yourself. Of course, there is always the risk when you do this rather than judge, that you may really get to like yourself.

5. Adult Children of Alcoholics have difficulty having fun.

6. Adult Children of Alcoholics take themselves very seriously.

Playing and having fun are wonderful goals to strive for. In a relationship, it may be important for you to say, "I am learning how to play and how to have fun. I want to do this a lot, because as a child I never learned how. If you will initiate, I will follow. I do not even know how to think of fun things to do, but I will do my best to go along with the things you suggest. Maybe in relatively short order, I will be ready to come up with some ideas, too." Having fun in a relationship is a superb priority to work on. But learning to have fun is serious business—for you.

Socializing is part of what many people in the "adult world" consider fun. You may even have to learn how to survive at a party.

Here's how some of my clients have expressed themselves on the subject of socializing.

"I have recently moved to a new city," John said. "I want very much to meet some people and make new friends. Although I want mainly a female, I would be satisfied right now if I could even meet a couple of guys to hang around with. I feel more lonely and isolated than usual, and I know it is up to me to do something about it. Last Saturday night there was an AA party in Boston, which is about half an hour away. I decided to go. I made the half-hour drive—pulled into the parking lot—parked my car—felt immediately depressed—turned on the ignition and drove home. When I feel depressed I am useless to myself or anyone else. It was not as if I could have bitten the bullet and went in anyway. I was finished."

Connie stated, "The anxiety I feel before I go somewhere is so overwhelming that I continually ask myself if it's worth going. I carry a complete make-up kit, manicure set and hair blower in my car, just in case I need to make one final stab at making myself look decent. If one hair is out of place, I know I will not be acceptable."

"When we were at that party last Sunday, you stayed pretty close to me most of the evening." Marie asked Jim, "Did you do that because you felt sorry for me?" She went on, "I would rather stay at home than go out socially. My own anxiety increases at a party, and by the end of an hour it overwhelms me, and I know I have to get out of there."

These are fairly typical COA reactions to a social situation. "Let's have a party" or "Let's go to a party" is met with enthusiasm, but with varying degrees of terror. Where does the terror come from? What does it mean? Can one learn to react differently? First, let me explain that COAs are not the only ones who experience anxiety when entering social situations, particularly those where they will encounter unfamiliar people. "What will I say?" "Will I be accepted?" "Do I look okay?" are universal concerns. I have never heard anyone say, "I adore cocktail party talk," or "It's great to go to a singles group," or "The bar scene is a boon to mankind." The reality is that social encounters are work for most people. Some enjoy them, some get by, but many just barely get through them. People who fortify themselves with chemicals are not usually capable of a realistic assessment until the following day. Certainly their anxieties were reduced, but their hilarious behaviors of the night before look different in the light of day.

COAs tend to react more strongly than others. Why is that? Back we go to those thrilling days of yesteryear. Parties—celebrations—holidays were all variations of the same theme. Going to a social event with your family generally caused embarrassment. You prayed that your alcoholic parent wouldn't get drunk. You tried to make yourself small enough so others wouldn't think you were with him/her. You worried about taking care of your alcoholic parent. You were desperate to leave before you even got there. Eventually, your family stopped going to parties. You became isolated.

Holidays were always a nightmare. You got all excited about Christmas or Thanksgiving and it would end up in a fight. You would be disappointed and upset. It was inevitable that something bad would happen. Your birthday might have been ignored; or if you had a party, you were in a panic. You could never be sure it would go okay. Having your friends visit your home was an unusual event, so the mere idea of it automatically produced anxiety.

Because of your increased isolation, you did not have much practice at social situations. Your parents were not available to teach you social skills. They did not show you how to dress, how to be comfortable, or how to talk to strangers. So no matter how appropriate and charming you appear to others, inside you feel you are fooling them all.

You believe that the attractive, well-dressed, charming, intelligent, warm person others see exists only in their imagination. This is what causes the depression or extreme anxiety over going to a party. It is a throwback to childhood and those traumatic, early experiences.

There are ways to make it easier if you decide to go:

1. Don't go alone. Go with a close friend.
2. Drive your own car.
3. Plan your exit before you get there.
4. Read the day's newspaper.
5. Find out if alcohol will be served.
6. Give yourself permission to be anxious.
7. Promise yourself you will meet one new person.
8. Be useful. Pass around the potato chips or help empty the ashtrays.
9. No matter what happens, congratulate yourself for making and following through on the decision to go.

Next time will be easier. All you need is some practice.

7. Adult Children of Alcoholics have difficulty with intimate relationships.

Recognize this as a truth. It is almost a universal truth. You are not the only one who has difficulty. Accept that fact. Intimate relationships are difficult for others, too; otherwise the number of divorces would not be so great.

Recognize the difficulty and make the decision that this is a hurdle which you are willing to work at to overcome. It sounds very simple, but it is not. Acceptance is never simple, but it gives you the freedom to change and enhance your life.

8. Adult Children of Alcoholics overreact to changes over which they have no control.

Harriet has been furious with Arthur for days, and cannot contain her anger at him. When they attended a dance a few nights ago, she put a lot of pressure on herself to have a good time, to participate and to become involved. When the disc jockey called out "Ladies' choice!" she said to herself, "Okay, I am going to be assertive and pick someone to dance with." Just as she had made this decision, Arthur came over and asked her to dance. She rudely turned him down and walked away. This incident took her back to her childhood, when her father had taken away her opportunities to do things for herself, her own way and to make her own mistakes. Because he was very dominant and domineering, she felt oppressed. These feelings surfaced when Arthur asked her to dance.

Since Harriet is a COA, in many ways she is compliant and will do as she is told. She makes the assumption that other people are also compliant, and will behave in the same manner. When the disc jockey said, "This is Ladies' Choice," she assumed that for everyone there it would be ladies' choice. However, Arthur was not compliant; he wanted to dance with her, and was not going to let the disc jockey decide for him.

Harriet had overreacted to a change over which she had no control. Arthur had taken it upon himself to change the rules. She, because of her overreaction, could not simply say to him, "Later. I want to do this differently right now."

It is important for you, as a COA, to recognize what you do to yourself when you react so strongly to a change. It does not mean that the person with whom you are involved is out to get you. It may simply mean that he does not follow the rules as you do, or that he is more spontaneous than you are. It is important for you to explain that you do not shift easily. That way, he will know that his ideas will not always be received by you in the way they are intended.

Developing flexibility is something you may want to work toward. You must realize that the desire and the ability to effect that change are two different things. Find out what is in your partner's head when he or she changes a rule. What you see as a personal affront may have a very different motive. It is only fair that you discover what the motive is, and clearly recognize that your response is not to the present incident, but to your past. Only then can you begin to reconcile these two things.

You may never be the easygoing, flexible, roll-with-it kind of person you would like to be, but it is a direction worth spending some time and energy on.

9. Adult Children of Alcoholics constantly seek approval and affirmation.

It is important that you recognize the excessive approval you seek from your partner. This can be a real trap for you in a relationship. Yet it is equally important for you to be involved with someone who affirms, validates and supports you. A healthy relationship involves two people who give each other the right to their feelings and the sense that they are of value. If your partner's

approval becomes paramount, you will begin to lose
yourself in the relationship. If it is necessary to your feeling good about yourself, you will be very easily manipu-
lated whenever that approval is withdrawn.

What you need is to seek your own approval. This does
not mean you do not want to please your partner, nor
that you won't feel wonderful when you do get approval.
But if you rely on another person for your sense of value,
you are no longer involved in an adult relationship. You
have allowed your partner to become a parent to you,
and say, "Yes, you are good, no, you are bad." For adults
this is not desirable.

When you find yourself in this situation, try to remember
that a parent-child relationship is not really what you want.
If you desire your partner to affirm you and tell you that you
are wonderful, that is different, as that is part of any healthy
relationship. It also helps you to approve of yourself more.
Primarily, you need to learn that the wonder of you exists
regardless of another person's acknowledgment.

10. Adult Children of Alcoholics usually feel different from other people.

Feeling different from other people seems to stay with
you throughout life. The sense of difference, aggravated

by your isolation as a child, is very hard to overcome. But feeling different does not have to continue to be a big deal, to carry with it components such as, "I am different because I am unworthy." You are different because you are unique, and you are developing your own personality.

In a relationship, don't pretend that you are not different, but begin to recognize your individuality, and also encourage your partner to celebrate his. This will enhance your own uniqueness as a couple. Though you may always feel different from other people, decide that it makes you more, and not less, interesting.

It is also time for you to realize that difference does not automatically mean worthless. We are all different. Growth enhances one's uniqueness, which does not mean that you are destined to be alone or lonely. It simply means that you are an individual in your own right.

11. Adult Children of Alcoholics are extremely loyal, even in the face of evidence that their loyalty is undeserved.

Your loyalty is one of your greatest assets, and one of your greatest liabilities. Anyone involved with you is very fortunate, because he/she can depend on you. You may run away from certain issues, but the loyalty you have for the people you care about knows no bounds. Although this is a wonderful quality, it needs to be tempered with rationality. You may continue to be loyal to someone whose behavior is inexcusable. Because of this unacceptable behavior, you may have to end a relationship or a friendship. It is critical to recognize the point at which you need to draw a line.

Loyalty to another person does not take precedence over everything else. Loyalty to yourself must come first. Ask yourself these questions: Am I getting out of this relationship what is good for me? Am I receiving to the degree that I am giving? Am I fantasizing that this relationship, because of my loyalty, will work out the way I want it to? This is a very important question. If, when you look at it realistically, it is less than you want, and the two of you are not willing to work out problems together, then you need to reassess. Walking away without trying to look at solutions is not a good idea. But neither is staying put because it's the only thing you know how to do. Your family was very loyal. However, the road to recovery began when that loyalty was tempered with reason and responsibility to each individual. Your loyalty to yourself must come first.

12. Adult Children of Alcoholics are either super-responsible or super-irresponsible.

One of the joys of being involved in a healthy relationship is that you don't have to handle everything by yourself. You can do your part and your partner can do his part. When problems arise, the two of you can sit down and work out a solution. It is important for you to recognize that you are not alone. Planning with another person is something new to you, but it takes a great deal of weight off your shoulders. No matter what is going on, there is someone you can discuss it with, someone you can include in finding ways to accomplish what you want to do. This is also true for your partner, who will include you in things that he/she wants to accomplish.

You are not alone. For example, if you are fixing a meal or running an errand, you can get help. If you have to figure out something which seems unsolvable, you can get help. You do not have to take all the responsibility. You can begin to balance your life. While you take care of some things, your partner can take care of others. You can participate, which is what a relationship is all about.

It will not be easy for you to trust that someone will be there for you, or to accept the fact that his/her word is good. It will not even be easy for you to believe that a problem is not wholly and completely yours. Yet, shared responsibility is essential to a healthy relationship.

If you are among those who are super-irresponsible, letting someone else do all the worrying and caring, another set of problems arises. You can probably find someone who takes pleasure in doing things for you. There are people who enjoy giving and who don't con-sider receiving important. Many of them, of course, are Adult Children of Alcoholics. What will happen even-tually is that if you don't become more responsible, your partner will learn to resent you. There is a limit to how much giving a person can do without getting anything in return.

So consider working on becoming more responsible. This, too, has its pitfalls. If you are involved with some-one who has decided to take care of you, you have entered into a parent-child role. When you decide to be more responsible, you may meet with resistance and resentment.

However, being irresponsible and having a healthy relationship are incompatible. You need to work on this trait, but you don't have to do it alone. If you are in a developing relationship and want to assume more responsibility, which has not been your style, talk it over. You can say, "I want to do more, to be an active participant, and I need your help." Relationships involve give and take. They are not one-sided.

13. Adult Children of Alcoholics tend to lock themselves into a course of action without giving serious consideration to alternative behaviors or possible consequences. This impulsivity leads to confusion, self-loathing and loss of control over the environment. As a result, much energy is spent cleaning up the mess.

Your impulsivity is one of your biggest enemies. If you feel compelled to make a phone call, fly to Europe, get married, end a relationship—put it off for a while. Call in an hour, decide on the European trip tomorrow, wait until the middle of the week to get engaged or to end a relationship. Once you have bought the time, force your-self to consider the alternatives and the consequences. If you cannot do that by yourself, find someone who can help you. Once you have considered the variables, you can make a reasonable decision (which may or may not be the one you had made impulsively). This is the only way you will be fully responsible for your actions. Later on, if things don't work out well, you won't say "if only."

If things do work out well, you will know it was not the result of fate, luck or chance, but of your own reasoning ability.

CONCLUSION

The family system affected by alcoholism is dysfunctional. Dysfunctional family systems have dysfunctional relationships. Your behavior is based upon what you learned as a child, but you don't want it for yourself. Knowing what you don't want does not mean you know what you *do* want.

You need to learn what a healthy relationship is.
You need to learn how to achieve one.
You need to change habits that do not work.
Struggle is inevitable.
Mistakes are inevitable.
Discouragement is inevitable.
However, so is—sharing, loving, enhancement, joy, excitement, companionship, understanding, cooperation, trusting, growth, security and serenity. The choice and the challenge are yours.

SUGGESTED READING

1. Harris, Dr. Thomas A. *I'm OK—You're OK*, New York: Harper & Row, 1967.

2. Paul, Jordan and Margaret Paul. *Do I Have to Give Up Me to Be Loved by You?* Minn.: CompCare, 1984.

3. Peck, M. Scott. *The Road Less Traveled*. New York: Simon & Schuster, 1978.

4. Pietsch, William V. *Human Be-Ing. How to Have a Creative Relationship Instead of a Power Struggle*. New York: Signet, 1974.

5. Vale Allen, Charlotte. *Daddy's Girl*. New York: Berkeley Books, 1980.

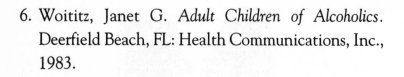

6. Woititz, Janet G. *Adult Children of Alcoholics.* Deerfield Beach, FL: Health Communications, Inc., 1983.

7. Woititz, Janet G. *Marriage on the Rocks*, Deerfield Beach, FL: Health Communications, Inc., 1979.

ABOUT THE AUTHOR

Janet Geringer Woititz, Ed.D., was the founder and President of the Institute for Counseling and Training in West Caldwell, New Jersey, which specialized in working with dysfunctional families and individuals. She was the author of the bestselling *Adult Children of Alcoholics* and *Struggle for Intimacy* as well as *Marriage on the Rocks, Healing Your Sexual Self* and *The Self-Sabotage Syndrome: Adult Children in the Workplace.* Her books are also available as tapes.

NOTES

More from the author

The Complete
ACoA Sourcebook

ADULT CHILDREN
OF ALCOHOLICS
at Home, at Work
and in Love

Janet Geringer Woititz, Ed.D.

with a foreword by
Robert Ackerman, Ph.D.
author, *Perfect Daughters*

Code #9608 • $16.95

Discover a guide to healthy living for anyone
whose life has been affected by dysfunction.